To Emily

hope

THE BIBLE STUDENT

THE BIBLE STUDENT

Edited by

Peter Sammons

Glory to Glory Publications

Contributors:
The Revs. Alex Jacob, David M. Moore and Peter Byron-Davies;
Greg Stevenson, Peter Sammons.

First published in Great Britain 2012 by
Glory to Glory Publications
an imprint of Buy Research Ltd
Glory to Glory Publications
PO Box 212 SAFFRON WALDEN CB10 2UU UK

www.glorytoglory.co.uk

ISBN 978-0-9567831-6-5

Printed in Great Britain
by CPI Group (UK) Ltd, Croydon, CR0 4YY

Contents

PREFACE

This book has been inspired by the fondly remembered *Every Man a Bible Student* which was originally published by the old Ruanda Mission (which later became the Mid-Africa Mission and finally incorporated into the CMS in 2002) and ran to a number of reprints during the following two decades. Many copies are still held and referred to. Joe Church's book is understood to have emerged during (and as a part of) the East African Revival of the 1930s, and it is believed that it was largely written in Rwanda.

The brevity, simplicity and biblical focus of the earlier volume remains its core strength. The contributors to this new book consciously referred to that earlier work, which has helped to shape the structure of these Studies, but this is a completely revised and re-ordered collection with the addition of some new topics. The purpose is to enable 'students' to get a sense of the majesty of the Bible and its internal consistency across so many difficult and sometimes perplexing issues. God works out his purposes through time and in different contexts but his message is timeless. We do well to try to discern his purposes as revealed in Scripture.

These studies are not 'lightweight', but are still within the capability of any diligent seeker to understand – especially as God the Holy Spirit helps those who seek to know Jesus better, the one who is *himself* the truth. Although the Bible references are many, readers are encouraged to work through them, and thereby to be blessed by the sheer excitement of hearing the living God speak!

It is the prayer of the contributors that these studies will be a real blessing and joy to all who use them. We have a wonderful Lord who has a wonderful purpose, revealed in his Word (that we call the Bible) and supremely in his Word – the Lord Jesus. This is no play on words: Jesus is the Word of God (e.g. John 1:1) but the Scriptures are also the Word of God given to all mankind.

It can be a daunting prospect to edit the work of others. These studies were prepared by five different Christians, but remain largely consistent in style, approach and theological understanding. Any errors in material must ultimately be the responsibility of the editor, and so it is in a humble but joyful spirit that these new studies are offered to a new generation.

To God be the glory, great things he has done....

Peter Sammons
Editor

EXPLANATION OF THE
BIBLE STUDY MATERIAL

This brief introduction is not intended to be exhaustive. There are many good books about the Bible, its history, dependability and inspiration. Bible study will be a lifetime's work for anyone serious about getting to grips with how God speaks to us through its pages. The purpose of this book is to provide specific studies based on particular themes. Obviously, the Bible is a large document and it can sometimes appear a daunting prospect to read and to study.

Two types of study can be helpful. *Firstly, a general reading of the books of the Bible.* We can ask the Holy Spirit to be our teacher and guide as we read large portions of the Scripture, even without the assistance of study notes and other prepared materials. By reading whole books at longer 'sittings' we can begin to appreciate the sweep of history and how God works out his purposes. Many books of the Bible, notably the epistles (letters), were clearly intended to be read in exactly that way. So this straightforward method of reading should not be neglected. There is an excellent case for consecutive reading of the whole Bible, so that we are not tempted to ignore passages that are unfamiliar or seem 'difficult' to us. *Secondly*, it can be helpful to *look at a particular theme* touching on: (a) God's revelation of himself; and (b) what it means to be a disciple of the Lord Jesus. It is this second method that is assisted by the materials in this book.

The Holy Bible – some basics

The Bible is divided into the Old Testament and the New Testament. These titles are not particularly helpful, suggesting that the Old is replaced by, or is somehow inferior to, the New. It tends to divide them when God has given both. Both speak of the same God. The God of Abraham, Isaac and Jacob is the same God and Father of the Lord Jesus Christ. We remember that the first generation of disciples only had what we call the Old Testament, with which they would have been very familiar, as well as the apostles' teaching which would later be collected and recognised as the New Testament.

The truly astonishing thing is that so many Old Testament prophecies have been fulfilled. God has made many promises in both Testaments and the experience of his faithful people is that he keeps his promises. That is one reason why studying the Old Testament remains so helpful today.

What shines through in both Testaments is mankind's desperate need for a redeemer, a Saviour – called the 'Messiah'; and God's provision for that need. Within the Old Testament there are hundreds of pointers towards the Messiah. The New Testament records the life, death and resurrection of that Messiah. His name as recorded in the New Testament, which was of course written in Greek, is transliterated into English as Jesus (Greek: *Yesous*), or rendered in Hebrew *Yeshua* (see Study No. 48).

Pitfalls to avoid

Understanding of the Bible is helped by considering the Bible as a whole. We should avoid looking for 'proof texts' to support a particular viewpoint. It is possible to take texts out of context, which is unhelpful or even misleading. In these notes, references are taken widely, from Genesis to Revelation, to give some sense of the whole. This enables a more panoramic view of the subject to be obtained. Only minimum explanation is given, so as to allow the texts to speak for themselves. Further notes are given where it is felt that additional explanation will be beneficial.

Quiet Time

It will probably be found useful and very helpful to study the Bible at times set aside for the purpose. This is sometimes referred to as a quiet time. If so, normally a quicker and more concentrated study is possible. Prayer and contemplation are also possible in a quiet time, and 'students' may find this a real blessing.

Questions

If you are new to Bible study, don't be afraid to ask searching questions. If you have a Christian friend who can help explain the Bible and any questions you have, then no doubt they will be more than glad to help you. But don't let go of your questions. You may find that by writing them down, even if you do not get an immediate answer, and coming back to them from time to time, other studies have helped to answer them, perhaps in unexpected ways. God gave us enquiring minds, so don't be afraid to use yours! As we get to know God more deeply, through his Son Jesus Christ (or Messiah), some hard questions will inevitably be raised. Never be afraid to ask questions and to search deeply. In this way you will progressively get to know how the Lord works and just how much he loves all those he has created. Ask the Holy Spirit to guide you in your study.

Basic principle

However far you feel you may be from God, he has shown his love for you by sending his Son, Jesus, to die on the cross and rise again, so you can respond to him, find forgiveness of sin through him, become a member of his body, live in him, persevere in the faith, and have life eternal. He wants you to know him personally, as Lord, Saviour, and friend. The prayer of those who have prepared these studies is that the Units will indeed help you to know him better by studying his word for yourself.

The Church

Followers of the Lord Jesus, searchers after God, are meant to find a home in a church. You will be mightily blessed by finding a Bible-believing church (and a 'church' is really a body of believers). You may have believing friends who can help you. If not, then do make enquiries to find out what sort of churches are located close to you. God will direct you to a church where you will feel at home and where you will grow as his follower. Again, ask the Holy Spirit to guide you.

Real encouragement!

As you become a true disciple (follower) of Jesus and come into the way of salvation – that is, if you are someone who has repented before God, and now believes in Jesus (who was crucified, and died, but today lives, as he was bodily raised from the dead) as your personal Lord and Saviour; and you are someone, moreover, who has 'nailed your colours to the mast' by being baptised as a public witness to your new life in Jesus – as you continue in that way of salvation, going on being filled with the Holy Spirit, and going on living in obedience to Jesus, you can rejoice in these wonderful truths. You are:

God's child (see John 1:12)
Christ's friend (see John 15:15)
Justified by faith (see Romans 5:1)
United with the Lord (see 1 Corinthians 6:17)
Bought with a price, and belong to God
(see 1 Corinthians 6:19–20)
A saint (see Ephesians 1:1)
Adopted as God's child (see Ephesians 1:5)

A believer can have confidence...

Has access by the Spirit to the Father (see Ephesians 2:18)
Has been redeemed (see Colossians 1:14)
Is complete in Christ (see Colossians 2:10)
Free from condemnation if in Christ Jesus and walking according to the Spirit, not the flesh (Romans 8:1–2)
Assured that all things work together for good to those who love God (see Romans 8:28)

and...

Cannot be separated from the love of Christ by persecution and other adversities (see Romans 8:35)
Has been sealed by God (see 2 Corinthians 1:21–22)
Is hidden with Christ in God (see Colossians 3:3)
Has citizenship of heaven (see Philippians 3:20)
Can have a spirit of power, love and self discipline (see 2 Timothy 1:7)
Can find grace and mercy in time of need (see Hebrews 4:16)

Our significance is in Christ

A believer is to be...

The salt and light of the earth (see Matthew 5:13–14)
A branch of the true vine (see John 15:5)
A personal witness of Christ (see Acts 1:8)
With other believers, God's temple (see 1 Corinthians 3:16) and one of God's co-workers (see 1 Corinthians 3:9)

and...

Has been chosen and appointed to bear fruit (see John 15:16)
Is seated with Christ in the heavenly places (see Ephesians 2:6)
Is God's workmanship (see Ephesians 2:10)
May approach God with freedom and confidence through faith in Christ (see Ephesians 3:12)
Can do all things through Christ (see Philippians 4:13)

Finally

You may live in a country where there are few churches or where the church is outlawed. Although you may not be able easily to enjoy fellowship and friendship with other brothers and sisters in Christ, the Lord Jesus will not abandon you if you have repented, given your life to him and go on believing in him. (See study No. 13.) He may well help you to discover Christian believers who are unknown to you – God does know who they are and where they are. Sooner or later he will give you the blessing of meeting and enjoying real fellowship with other true believers in Jesus. Your task is to go on believing in him. He will sustain you!

1
SIN

Background

How can sin be described? It is, in a very real sense, putting yourself at the centre of everything, as in sIn, where 'I' or 'me' is the operative word. God is left on the periphery – if he features at all! Sin is rebellion against God (consciously or unconsciously) and ultimately it is enmity with God. It can be seen in three distinct ways:

* by act – e.g. theft is an act of sin
* by attitude – e.g. jealousy is an attitude of sin
* by state – e.g. being unsaved is a state of sin

Human beings are by their very nature separated from a holy and loving God. Separated by act, by attitude and by spiritual condition. Sin, at its most basic, is rebellion against God's right to be God over our lives. Generally speaking, humans resent not being at the centre, and rebel against the One who should be central in our lives – the Lord Jesus.

Origins of sin – what the Bible says

Christians believe that it is only in the Holy Bible that the origin of sin is adequately revealed. The reality of sin in the world is difficult to deny, although many try to do so, trying to blame humanity's conditions for the world's problems – or even blaming God himself! The scarlet stain of sin runs through all the books of the Bible:

Genesis **2**:17; **3**:4–13, 18, 19; **13**:13; Numbers **32**:23; Psalm **51**:5; Proverbs **14**:9; Isaiah **1**:5, 6; **14**:12–14; Mark **7**:20–23

Sins of act

Galatians **5**:17–21

Sins of attitude

Matthew **5**:21, 22, 28; **23**:28; Psalm **66**:18; Luke **18**:11–14; James **2**:8–9

Sins of state

John **16**:8, 9; James **4**:17; Romans **7**:1–12; 1 Corinthians **15**:21–22; 1 John **1**:5, 8; **3**:4, 8; **5**:17–19

Sin is universal

By nature humans are born in a state of sin, which is the natural inclination of all mankind, even those who have been born again. See John **13**:10 – the reference to having had a bath represents salvation; the reference to washing of feet represents the periodic need even of believers to repent of specific, known sins.

Having been 'born in sin' does not mean that babies have committed particular sins, but that there is an inevitability that they will sin as they grow older. They will push back at God's right to be God of their lives.

Sin is a terminal disease of the soul and must be completely cleansed if we are to avoid what is only justice – eternal punishment following judgement by a righteous God.

Cleansing, forgiveness happens both at one distinct, definite moment in an act of commitment to Jesus as Lord and Saviour, as we hand our lives and our futures over to him – and we are saved from the penalty of past sins – and also on an ongoing basis. Our old nature will periodically try to reassert itself, and we will need to go on asking for forgiveness for particular sins. Committing our lives to Jesus is, and must be, an act of repentance, an act of turning to Jesus and away from sin. This is a life-changing event, normally at baptism, (but sometimes before baptism) and thereafter as the need arises – probably daily! Sin is like a burden. If not released from it, the burden will inevitably drag us down and affect our physical, mental and often social and economic well-being. Ultimately it will be judged. Jesus alone amongst all the humans who have ever lived was without sin.

Romans **3**:9, 23; **5**:12; **7**:24–25; Acts **17**:26; Ephesians **2**:1–3; Hebrews **4**:15; 1 John **3**:5

1 Peter **2**:22; Genesis **3**:8–10; 23–24; **6**:7; Isaiah **48**:22; Joshua **7**:10–12; 25–26

The remedy for sin was prepared from the beginning of time

In the Old Testament the blood of a sacrificed animal made 'atonement' for the man who offered the animal, if he truly repented (that means, turned away from his sin) and believed in the sufficiency of the sacrificed blood. At the right time God came himself, in the form of Jesus, the 'Son of Man', the 'Lamb of God', and voluntarily died once for all, for the sins of the world. Since Jesus' death for us, belief in Jesus and more particularly *in his blood shed for us*, is the only way to escape from the power and the consequences of sin ('the wages of sin is death'). The ultimate consequence of sin is eternal punishment in hell (see especially Jesus' teaching in the Gospels on this topic), which also entails eternal separation from God.

Ezekiel **18**:4, 20; Isaiah **1**:13–18; Acts **4**:12; **13**:38; John **1**:29; Hebrews **9**:26–28; 1 John **1**:7

Romans **5**:19; **6**:11–12, 23.

2
REPENTANCE

Background

Repentance means more than saying sorry. It means a genuine turning away from the sins that we have committed, asking God's forgiveness and making up our minds that we want to follow God's way when we next face the temptation to sin (for information on sin, see Study No. 1). True repentance means a radical change of mind, and genuine sorrow for sin. This is a 'change of heart', as well as an act – the act of formally asking for God's forgiveness. Feeling remorse, or 'doing penance', are in themselves not real repentance.

The Bible gives clear teaching about the confession of sin, whether public or private:

Confession is to God

It acknowledges that the sin is against God.

Psalm **32**:5 – *Then I acknowledged my sin to you and did not cover up my iniquity. I said, "I will confess my transgressions to the Lord" – and you forgave the guilt of my sin.*

Psalm **51**:4 – *Against you, you only, have I sinned and done what is evil in your sight.*

Confession is vital

–but not necessarily public: God's promise of forgiveness depends on confession as part of repentance. (See 1 John **1**:9.)

Confession to the one wronged?

– if possible, though this should always be done with great sensitivity and, if unsure how to proceed, the advice of a trusted Christian friend or minister should be sought (Numbers **5**:6–7).

Confession of sins to other Christians

James taught that we should confess our sins to one another (James **5**:16). Jesus taught that repentance, and sometimes restitution, are necessary before coming to him (Matthew **5**:23–24). This seems to refer to situations where an injured party knows he has been wronged. So, if he suspects nothing, it could do more harm to tell him, for example, of hateful thoughts that you previously felt towards him.

Matthew **21**:28–31; **27**:3–5; 2 Samuel **12**:13–18; Psalm **51**:10; Luke **15**:17, 18, 20; Acts **8**:21–22; 2 Corinthians **7**:9–10

Repentance must precede the new birth

(See John **3**:1–16.)

Repentance is the key that opens the door through which a person enters by faith into eternal life. Saving faith is impossible without repentance.

Matthew **3**:2, 8; **4**:17; **9**:13; Luke **24**:47, 48; Acts **2**:38; **17**:30; **20**:20–21; **26**:19–20

Unwillingness to repent blinds a person

and eventually hardens his or her conscience.

Matthew **11**:15, 20, 22; 1 John **1**:6, 8, 10; Isaiah **1**:13–15; Hebrews **6**:6; Luke **13**:3

God repeatedly warns the unrepentant person

—but God's arms are always outstretched to receive the penitent.

Ezekiel **18**:31–32; 2 Corinthians **5**:20 and **6**:2; Luke **15**:7; **15**:20; Revelation **2**:5, 16, 21; **3**:3, 19; Romans **10**:21

Summary

True repentance is essential if humans are to find peace with God. True repentance necessarily involves a change of mind – a change of heart. God is completely righteous so he will ultimately judge sin. But he has provided a complete and permanent remedy for sin: the sacrifice Jesus made on the cross for our sins. We are to repent of (turn away from) our sins, have a real, complete change of heart, believe and trust in Jesus Christ as Lord and Saviour, and then go on believing and trusting in him.

God promises that as we ask him he will fill us with his Holy Spirit. He will go on helping us to overcome whenever we are tempted to sin again. That is a truly amazing thought.

3
FAITH

Background

What is faith? Faith can be described as complete and unreserved trust (a) in God, as the one who fulfils his promises contained in his word; and (b) in Jesus the Messiah (Christ) as Saviour and Lord. Faith helps us to see the reality of the unseen. It is the continuing attitude of the genuine Christian.

God has shown himself to be completely trustworthy. We trust the Son of God, Jesus Christ, because he led the life of perfection, showing us how we are meant to live in obedience. The Lord Jesus paid the debt we owe through our rebellion against God (sin) and he did it by living a sinless life and dying on the cross in our place. We trust God's Son because he went willingly and knowingly to the Cross – the perfect sacrifice for all mankind, and the perfect sacrifice for each of us as individuals. We trust because God keeps his promises. We trust because God has loved each and every human being, despite the sins that so often spoil. How has he loved us? By giving Jesus his Son to stand in our place. His love is not because we are good or 'lovable'. Because of his mercy he has provided that undeserved gift. His will is that each one of us should not continue to be a slave to sin, but that (through Jesus) we should be saved from the penalty, the power and the consequences of sin. Christian believers are encouraged by answered prayer and by the power and godliness we see displayed in the lives of others who have put their faith in Jesus.

We therefore have good reason for our faith. God desires that our faith should increase — and this does seem to be the pattern, over time, for those who walk closely with him, in his ways.

In the Old Testament

Salvation through faith appears a number of times. There is also real faith in God's repeated promises and 'agreements' (more correctly called 'covenants'). The following are some Old Testament verses on faith and New Testament commentary on them:

Genesis **6**:22; **12**:1–5; **13**:14–18   cf. Hebrews **11**:7–10

Genesis **15**:6   cf. Romans **4**:2–5; Hebrews **11**:11–12.

Genesis **22**:1–19   cf. Hebrews **11**:17–19.

Genesis **50**:24, 25   cf. Hebrews **11**:22

Exodus **9**:20, 21; Exodus **12**:21–25   cf. Hebrews **11**:28

Joshua **6**:20   cf. Hebrews **11**:30

Ruth **2**:12; Psalms **56**:3

In the New Testament

Jesus Christ claimed to fulfil Old Testament promises. Accordingly, faith was to be placed in him from that time forwards.

Matthew **16**:8; Mark **6**:5–6; **9**:23; **10**:52; Luke **7**:50; **8**:50; **17**:5–6, **22**:32

John **1**:12; **3**:15–16, 36; **6**:35–36; **7**:38; **8**:24; **11**:25–26; **12**:46

The Apostles went out into the world with this one message: *". . . believe on the Lord Jesus and you will be saved"* (Acts **16**:31).

Acts **3**:16; **4**:12; **8**:5, 35; **10**:43; Romans **3**:21–22; **5**:1–2; **10**:4, 9; 1 Corinthians **1**:23; **2**:2; 2 Corinthians **4**:5

Galatians **2**:15–16, 20; **3**:22; 2 Thessalonians **1**:3; 1 Peter **1**:8, 21; **2**:7

We are saved by grace through faith

But the fruit of this faith will be demonstrated in the works of our lives. Faith in itself has no merit – it is, figuratively speaking, the hand that takes the salvation that God gives.

Romans **4**:1–5; **10**:9–10; James **2**:14, 16, 24; Titus **3**:4–8; Galatians **2**:21; Ephesians **2**:8–10 (RV); **6**:16

1 Timothy **6**:12; 1 John **5**:4

Biblical Summary

The 'cloud of witnesses' who lived and died by faith.

Hebrews **12**:1–2 (cf. chapter 11)

4
ATONEMENT

Background

Atonement is the act by which God and man are brought together in personal relationship. The word in English is derived from Anglo-Saxon words meaning 'making at one'. Hence, some have rendered it 'at-one-ment'. It presupposes a separation – indeed alienation – that must be overcome if we are to know God and have fellowship with him. The word 'atonement' is translated from the Old Testament 'Kaphar' (to cover), meaning that sins have been covered over by the blood of the sacrifice. In theology, the word 'atonement' has come to include the whole idea of redemption through the Blood of Christ. The word is used once in the New Testament, in Romans **5**:11 (Authorised Version), but tends in modern translations to be translated as 'reconciliation' which is possibly a clearer word in modern language.

The need for atonement, or reconciliation, is bound up with man's thorough addiction to sin. All of scripture points to our sin. Some examples follow:

Isaiah **53**:6 – *all we like sheep have gone astray*

Jeremiah **17**:9 – *the heart is deceitful above all things, and desperately corrupt, who can understand it?*

Psalm **14**:3 – *there is none that do good, no, not one*

Romans **3**:23 – *all have sinned and fall short of the glory of God*

The apostle Paul described men as *enemies of God* (Romans **5**:10), *hostile to God* (Romans **8**:7), and *estranged and hostile in mind* (Colossians **1**:21)

In Old Testament times

−sins were covered by God in anticipation of the Cross. Sacrifice was the remedy for sin, and a man would sacrifice not only for his own sins but also for the sins of his family. Having truly repented, he would sacrifice an innocent animal − and always an animal without blemish. He trusted that God would fulfil his promise by cleansing him from his sin, if he offered blood.

Exodus **30**:10; Hebrews **10**:4; Leviticus **1**:3−4; **4**:27−31; **16**:11, 17, 30; **17**:11; **23**:27

Animal sacrifices were in anticipation of the sacrifice of Jesus

In a sense they might be thought of as foreshadowing the death of Jesus Christ.

Hebrews **10**:1; John **1**:29; 1 John **2**:2; Hebrews **9**:13−15, 22, 26; **10**:10, 14; Romans **3**:25; **8**:3; 1 Corinthians **5**:7

Now, under grace, having repented of sins, and having faith in the blood of Jesus shed for us, we are reconciled to God. Atonement has been made. Reconciliation is achieved through the blood of Jesus. His blood was the necessary price to be paid for the redemption of the world. It is really no exaggeration, then, to say that Christ's death was the supreme moment, the supreme event, in the history of the world.

Mark **10**:45; John **10**:11; Romans **3**:21−25; **5**:10, 11; 2 Corinthians **5**:21; Ephesians **1**:7; 1 Peter **1**:18−19; 1 John **4**:10

Notes

Terms that may be used in describing the atonement:

Representative – Christ's death was representative (see Hebrews **2**:14–17 and Romans **5**:19).

Propitiatory – Christ's death makes us what would otherwise be impossible – it makes us acceptable to God (see 1 John **4**:10).

Vicarious – Christ's death was a substitute, because he died in our place – in the place of the sinner (see Isaiah **53**:5–6, and 1 Peter **2**:24).

5
SACRIFICE

Background

In Old Testament times sacrifice involved the slaying of an innocent animal for the guilt of the individual on whose behalf the animal was killed. Where this act of slaying (in the manner laid down in the Law) was accompanied by true repentance and faith, God looked upon the blood that had been shed, in anticipation of the cross of Christ, and granted atonement.

As we think about sacrifice of the innocent animal, we need to remember the high cost of sin, and be grateful that the need for physical sacrifice was removed once and for all (literally once and literally for all) by the Lord Jesus' sacrifice on the cross.

The Old Testament

True sacrifice as ordained by God in the Old Testament

was the shadow, of which Christ's death was the reality. But Cain's unauthorised sacrifice, which God rejected, was the forerunner of the almost universal 'sacrifice' of humans to idolatry and immorality.

Genesis **4**:3, 5; **8**:20; **22**:8, 13; **31**:54; **46**:1; Exodus **18**:12; **12**:3–13; Leviticus **1**:2–4; ch. **16**; Deuteronomy **32**:16–17; 1 Samuel **15**:22; Proverbs **17**:1 (AV, UK); Hebrews **11**:4; **10**:1; 1 Corinthians **10**:20

Two things were necessary for Atonement under the Law:

1. Faith – in the offering of the blood sacrifice.

2. Repentance – Isaiah **1**:13, 16, 18; Numbers **5**:7 (confession and, where possible, restitution).

An important part of the sacrificial system was ceremonial washing. This requirement showed the necessity for cleansing from the impurity of sin. It was in a real sense the forerunner of Christian baptism which symbolizes the 'washing' away of sin. See, for example, Leviticus **14**:8–9; Numbers **8**:7; **19**:13; also Acts **22**:16.

The New Testament

The lamb was quintessentially the animal of sacrifice. See e.g. Genesis **22**:13, the lamb that God would provide was ultimately the Lord Jesus. The New Testament period opens with John the Baptist's triumphant cry *Behold the Lamb of God!* (John **1**:36). The Holy Bible ends, in the book of Revelation, with a vision of the glory of the *Lamb that was slain from the creation of the world* (Revelation **13**:8).

John **1**:36; **3**:16; 1 Corinthians **5**:7; Hebrews **9**:13-14; Revelation **13**:8

(Note: there is a compelling case that the Lamb of God should more correctly be translated the 'Ram' of God. The ram that would be sacrificed was a grown ram in the prime of its life, having lived a useful life. It was something of real value to its owner and involved a real cost to him to offer it in sacrifice. The shadow of Christ is seen in Genesis **22**:13 –and here the animal to be sacrificed is described emphatically as a ram. The Lord Jesus, when he was sacrificed on the cross for our sins, was also in his prime of life [assumed age of about thirty-three years], having lived a truly sinless life.)

The sacrifice of Christ for the sin of the world was final

There is no other way, and no other true gospel. The veil in the Jewish temple in Jerusalem was torn from top to bottom, a vivid demonstration that the way to God is now open for all. Indeed, before Christians were known as 'Christians', they were known as the people of the Way. From the earliest times of the church, Christians have considered offerings of animals or incense as completely ineffective. They rightly accept only the 'sacrifice' of prayer, of praise and of thanksgiving, with a genuine, humble and contrite heart, as being acceptable acts of thanksgiving before a righteous, saving God. As there are no more atoning sacrifices, it follows that there can be no priests (*sacerdotes*). In any case, the Jewish temple was soon to be destroyed (by the Romans in AD 70) and the old priesthood no longer exists. Instead God has created in those who truly believe in the Lord Jesus a royal priesthood – the priesthood of all believers (1 Peter **2**:9).

John **10**:18; **12**:32–33; **17**:4; **19**:30; Romans **3**:25; **5**:9; 1 Corinthians **6**:20; 2 Corinthians **5**:19; Galatians **3**:13; Ephesians **1**:7; Colossians **1**:21–22; Hebrews **9**:12; **10**:10–18; 1 Peter **1**:18–19; **2**:24

Two things are necessary for atonement under grace:

1. *Faith* in the offering of the blood of Jesus (see Romans **3**:24–25; Hebrews **10**:12).

2. *Repentanc*e a conscious turning away from sin and a determination to live a life acceptable to God. Literally a change of mind, not so much about individual plans, intentions or beliefs, but rather a change in a personality until now oriented towards sin, but in future oriented towards God (Acts **20**:21). Such penitence is not an isolated act but a disposition of mind, encouraging a change of behaviour and including where necessary, acts of reparation (See Luke **19**:8).

Christian baptism is a symbol of the cleansing of the heart from sin

See again the note above on Old Testament ceremonial washing.

1 Peter **3**:20–21   [See also Unit 31 on baptism.]

According to the Roman Catholic Church, the sacrament of penance includes the elements of contrition, confession and satisfaction. The priest is then empowered to pronounce absolution. However, in the New Testament there is no linkage between a 'sacramental framework' and absolution by a human priest. Indeed, this idea is inconsistent with the need for a sinner to turn personally to God in penitence, and receive absolution through Christ the only mediator (1 Timothy **2**:5) who is the great High Priest of his people.

6
REDEMPTION

Background

'Redemption' is an English word from a Latin root meaning to 'buy back'. It is the liberation of any person or possession by payment of a ransom. In the Christian theological context, redemption means freeing from the slavery of sin, and the ransom price paid for that freedom. This thought is most readily expressed in the Gospels, where Christ came to give his life as a ransom for many (Matthew **20**:28; Mark **10**:45). A sinner can be delivered from the bondage of Satan, sin and death, by the precious blood of Jesus, which is the purchase price. Jesus is both the *Redeemer* and the *ransom*.

In the Old Testament

– the *kinsman redeemer* is a fore-shadow of Christ our Redeemer. There are two essential parts to this: he has to be able to pay the price in full and he has to be a kinsman.

Leviticus **25**:25, 27, 48–49; Ruth **3**:12–13; **4**:4–6; Job **19**:25; Psalm **19**:14; Isaiah **59**:20

Note that in the Old Testament the object of God's redemption is generally the people as a whole, or nation, rather than individuals. The beginning of this idea of national redemption is the freeing of the Israelites from the bondage of slavery in Egypt. Though they were in bondage, God redeemed them (Exodus **6**:6; Deuteronomy **15**:15). The main difference here, however, is that in these redemptions, a price was not paid, as God redeems by his own might (Isaiah **52**:3).

In the New Testament

– we see the fulfilment by Jesus of the Old Testament 'types' (as in 'prototypes'). In Greek three words are used and translated as 'redeemer':

(a) *agorazo* – to purchase IN the slave market
(b) *exagorazo* – to buy OUT OF the slave market
(c) *lutroo* – to pay the ransom for, and so to redeem from the death of slavery

Mark **10**:45; Luke **1**:68; Acts **20**:28; Romans **3**:10, 19, 24; **7**:14; **8**:2; 1 Corinthians **1**:30; **7**:22–24

2 Corinthians **5**:14–17; Ephesians **1**:7, 14; Galatians **3**:10; **4**:4–5; 1 Timothy **2**:6; Titus **2**:14

The **purchase price** is not money. It is the **blood of the Redeemer**, shed for us on the cross at Calvary. We are redeemed from 3 things:
- Guilt
- Penalty
- Dominion (of sin)

Psalm **49**:15; Matthew **20**:28; John **1**:29; 2 Corinthians **5**:21; Galatians **3**:13; 1 Peter **1**:18–19; Revelation **5**:9

The motivating force behind redemption

is the love of God. The one who believes in Jesus will be freed from the bondage of sin, and find favour again with his Redeeming God. (See John **3**:16.)

There are, however, **three essential conditions to be complied with**. The enslaved man must:
- believe in his Redeemer (Jesus)
- believe in the price as sufficient (the blood of Jesus)
- get up and leave his bondage

The freed slave need never again be exposed for sale.

Psalm **31**:5; Isaiah **43**:1; John **3**:18–19; **8**:32; Acts **8**:13, 21–23; Romans **6**:20–23; **8**:2; Galatians **4**:31; **5**:13; Hebrews **2**:14–15

7

JUSTIFICATION

Background

What is 'justification'?

It is judicial acquittal – being found not guilty. Wherever the word 'justification' is found in the New Testament, the substitution of the word 'acquittal' can be a precise alternative. The word is used in the Old Testament in relation to human justice – e.g. Isaiah **5**:23 and Proverbs **17**:15, although here again some modern translations use the word 'acquit'. Justification is the gracious *finding innocent* of the true believer. It is a free gift from God given to those who believe in Jesus – it is the Judge himself who declares the believer not guilty. In Christianity a true believer is found not guilty because the penalty for their sins has been borne by Jesus.

Justification means more than forgiveness

It is a term which belongs in a court of law. An accused person is either condemned or justified – enquiries into his actions lead to him being found either *not guilty* or *guilty* of having broken the law. An innocent person is a just person, and the judge who proves a person 'just' is said to justify him. Another modern word that gives a similar sense is *vindication*. Justification does not make the sinner any different: it declares him just in the eyes of the law. The sinner certainly needs to be made good, and the Holy Spirit will go on helping to achieve that in the lives of believers, in what is known as 'sanctification'. Justification has to do not with our state but with our standing – it refers to our position before God. Apart from Christ we have no standing at all; we are guilty and condemned. But with Christ as our Saviour and substitute we are justified and acquitted – for Jesus has borne our sin himself.

Isaiah **50**:8; John **5**:24; Romans **3**:19, 20, 25, 26; **4**:5, 8; **8**:31–34; 1 Corinthians **1**:30; 2 Corinthians **5**:21

Believers are justified because Jesus Christ has borne their sins on the cross.

God, as Judge, declares that those who believe in Christ as their Saviour are justified and righteous.

Romans **4**:25; **5**:9; **8**:1

Justification is entirely a work of grace

It is unmerited and, in the words of the apostle Paul, not by any *works of righteousness* which we have done. Good works, pleading, self-sacrifice and giving all one's goods are of no eternal value.

John **3**:17–18; Romans **3**:24, 28–30; **5**:16–18; Galatians **2**:16; **3**:8, 11, 24; **5**:4; Luke **18**:14

We must admit our guilt before the completely righteous judge

Only then can we be justified by faith. Afterwards our lives must bear witness to our faith.

Ephesians **2**:8–10; Titus **3**:4, 5, 7; James **2**:21–24; 1 John **1**:9

Conclusion

Justification and righteousness have a similar meaning in many instances in scripture. Romans **5**:1–11 is a good summary of the joyful effect of justification (or acquittal) before God.

The concept of 'justification' should be considered alongside the meaning of 'righteousness'. We need to consider especially the complete and holy righteousness of God.

8

THE GOSPEL

Background

The word 'Gospel' means 'good news'. In the English language the word derives from two ancient Anglo-Saxon words '*God*' [good] and '*spell*' [story]. In English translations of the Bible, the expression 'good news' is sometimes used to denote all that Jesus has done. The good news is the glad tidings of salvation – it is about something that has happened which can benefit all mankind. The Greek word often translated 'gospel' or 'good news' is *euangelion*, from which we have the word 'evangelise' [proclaim the good news about Jesus]. One writer explains the original significance of the word thus:

> Very often in the Roman empire there was a big war going on at some distant boundary, and the people waited, breathless, in the city of Rome, for news of the battle, to hear whether it had been won or lost. If it had been won, the messenger would come running into Rome, shouting, 'Gospel, gospel, gospel!' And he meant victory. Good news: the battle is over and it has been won. That is what the word gospel means. It does not just mean something nice to hear or a good story, or even the story of God, it means this: a battle has been fought and we can now announce the victory — peace can be ours. . . . In the very first part of the Gospel [Mark], the battle is shown to be between God and Satan. That is the warfare. That battle was engaged two thousand years ago, and the victory has been won by God — the beginning of the Gospel, the good news of victory. How did it all take place? Where was the warfare engaged? The answer is: in a man called Jesus Christ, who was also the Son of God . . . . [© David Pawson *Come with me through Mark*, 2009. Used by permission]

Salvation (*from* the penalty of sin; *into* eternal life) is promised to those who repent, believe in Jesus, are baptised, and go on believing and trusting him, abiding in him. The good news is entrusted to Christ's followers, who are to tell others about that salvation, about atonement, about the crucifixion of Jesus for our sins, about his resurrection from the dead, and about the new birth which marks the beginning of a new life 'in Christ', which is possible for each and every man and woman – and indeed every child, too.

Note that there is a distinction to be made (generally indicated by capitalisation of the initial letter) between a 'Gospel' and 'the gospel'. The former denotes each of the four canonical Gospels (Matthew, Mark, Luke and John, respectively) whilst the term 'the gospel' signifies the heart of the apostolic message (e.g. in Romans **15**:1, where Paul writes of, 'the gospel which I preached to you . . . .' The true apostolic gospel is elsewhere contrasted with a false 'gospel' to which some were turning; see Galatians **1**:6.)

The promise of a Saviour and Redeemer of the world runs through the pages of the Old Testament

In Genesis **22**:15 – 18, God promises faithful Abraham that through his seed all nations shall be blessed. Whilst the first application is to the ancient people of God, we can see how the blessing of people of all nations is happening as salvation through Jesus Christ is being made known worldwide. (See also Galatians **3**:8 in the New Testament.) See Isaiah **9**:2, 6 – 7 in which the birth of Jesus is foretold, and especially Isaiah **53**. Other Old Testament passages can be read as having messianic significance in the light of the New Testament.

Jesus the Messiah, when he came to the world, claimed to fulfil God's promises

See Isaiah **61**:1–2; Luke **4**:16–21; Matthew **3**:1–2; **4**:23; Mark **1**:15; **8**:35; **10**:29–30; Luke **2**:10; **9**:6. Christ's followers are commissioned to proclaim him throughout the world. Only after Jesus has been proclaimed to 'the ends of the earth' shall the end of this world come. Many Christians today believe that the ease of communications stemming from globalisation and modern media mean that we are rapidly reaching the time when the gospel will indeed be accessible throughout the world. Accordingly, they expect active opposition to church and gospel to accelerate and to reach new levels of intensity.

See Matthew **24**:14; Mark **13**:10; **16**:15; Acts **8**:1–4 and v. 25; **13**:1–4; **14**:21; **15**:7; **16**:9–10; Romans **1**:1 and v. 16; **15**:18–20; 1 Corinthians **1**:17; **9**:12; 2 Corinthians **10**:16.

Jesus taught that after his death and resurrection the Holy Spirit would be sent. Then the disciples would be enabled to proclaim the gospel to the world. See John **14**:16 and 26; **15**:26–27; **16**:7 and vv. 13–14.

See also: Romans **2**:16; **16**:25; 1 Corinthians **1**:17; **9**:17–18; Ephesians **3**:1–8; **6**:19; Acts **20**:24; 1 Thessalonians **1**:5; **2**:2; Revelation **14**:6.

There are two key warnings in relation to the gospel. Firstly, any other 'gospel' is evil. Secondly, we are told that the true good news will not be accepted by everyone. Sadly, some will reject it. See Matthew **13**:1–23. Some would be mistaken and fall into error. See Galatians **1**:6–9; **2**:11–14; Colossians **2**:16–18; 2 Corinthians **11**:1–4 and vv. 13–15.

The apostle Paul said, 'Woe to me if I do not preach the gospel!' (1 Corinthians **9**:16). It is vital that Christians tell others the good news of salvation. The eternal destinies of the unsaved depend on this good news, and Christians themselves miss great blessings if they fail to proclaim it.

9
FORGIVENESS

Background

In human terms forgiveness carries with it the idea of ceasing to feel anger or resentment against a wrong. Of pardon, or of being 'let-off' a debt that is owed. The deepest meaning of forgiveness in Scripture means the separation of the sinner from his sin. It goes deeper than the human idea possibly can. Forgiveness means, fundamentally, that the one against whom a wrong has been done decides not to hold that against the wrongdoer, and will exact no penalty for it. The wrong may be a sin against God himself or against a fellow human being (or both, as in the case of murder, for example, which is clearly a wrong against the victim and a sin against God's law). Simply to fail to love our Creator – or to disobey his law – is to sin against him, and is something, therefore, that needs to be forgiven.

When God forgives a sin there is relief from a load that has been carried. Above all, it means that the penalty for the sin does not have to be paid by the sinner. Forgiveness does not mean that the (forgiven) sin has no consequences in this world – sadly consequences may continue. The New Testament Greek word translated 'forgiveness' is '*aphiemi*' ('send away'). As we saw in Study No. 7, the forgiven sinner is 'justified' before God. The one forgiven may then say: 'It is as if I'd never sinned in the first place.' Of course, sinful lifestyles must be abandoned. Jesus says to a forgiven sinner, '...go and sin no more' (John **8**:11b). A forgiven person is wise to avoid occasions of future temptation, especially if there is what some call a 'besetting sin'.

Old Testament

To whom can forgiveness be granted? In the Old Testament, the individual man or woman, truly repenting of sin (which would include confession, and restitution where the sin had been committed against another person) could be granted forgiveness. A blood sacrifice, in compliance with the law (*Torah*) would often be made, upon which forgiveness by God was granted. However, 'the blood of bulls and goats cannot take away sin'. The sacrifices in the Old Testament foreshadow the greater (final) sacrifice that would one day be made by Jesus. See Leviticus **4**:20, 26; **5**:10, 18 (details of sin offerings required); Numbers **15**:25–26 (priests could make sacrifice for the community); Psalms **32**:5; **66**:18; **103**:12 (the necessity to turn away from – to repent of – sin is emphasised); Isaiah **44**:22 (God redeemed his people, swept away their offences and called them to return to him). In Jeremiah **31**:33–34 we are shown that a time was to come when God's law would be written on the hearts of his people and they would know him personally, and know his forgiveness.

New Testament

The sacrifices of the Old Testament are completed in Jesus. (See Hebrews **9**:22 – 28.) Jesus said, "*This is my blood of the new covenant, which is poured out for many for the forgiveness of sins*" (Matthew **26**:28). See also Matthew **9**:2, 5–6. This is confirmation of Jesus' ministry to take away the sin of the world (John **1**:29). It should be noted, however, that Jesus takes away the sins of the truly penitent. The sins of the impenitent remain.

Forgiveness is by the grace of God

'Grace' signifies that when forgiveness is granted it is a gift given *freely* (i.e. Christ has paid the penalty of sin, dying that we might live) but this does not mean that it is 'unconditional'. There is a need to truly repent, and the need to believe 'on'

Jesus as the one who has paid the debt (taken the penalty) for one's sin. The 'on' in that sentence signifies far more than intellectual assent to propositions about Jesus, it also means personal, practical trusting in him, faithfulness to him, believing and acknowledging that his sacrifice, his death and resurrection really was for *you*, to take away *your* own sins and bring *you* into his way. True repentance is not merely feeling sorry. It includes stopping doing the sin, turning *away* from the sinful way of behaving, and turning *to* Christ! True repentance is not present or possible if we ourselves are unwilling to forgive. See Matthew **6**:12, 14, 15; **18**:21–35; Luke **17**:3–4. See also Romans **3**:24; **4**:7; Ephesians **4**:32; Colossians **2**:13; **3**:13; Acts **10**:43; 1 John **1**:7; **2**:2. Unforgiveness towards others will be punished (see again Matthew **18**:21–35). God, in his true 'agape' love, is willing and ready to forgive completely a truly repentant sinner. It is ultimately our decision whether we receive that divine forgiveness or reject what is offered. Remember that, 'this is the day of salvation' – so tomorrow may be too late (see 2 Corinthians **6**:1–2).

Final thoughts

Since only the one true God is holy, only he can forgive sins (Mark **2**:7; Luke **5**:21). We see Jesus' true divinity as in his earthly ministry he forgave sins. All sin is ultimately against God (e.g. Psalm **51**:4). Forgiveness of sins is not available from the other 'gods', nor from the world's non-Christian religions. Even as a concept in discourse about other religions it does not carry the same meaning. For example, in animism there is no personal relationship with (nor awareness of a responsibility to) the only true and living God. Hinduism demands that all must suffer inexorable consequences in their supposed 'wheel' of reincarnations – and offers no hope of forgiveness. Buddhism does not know a forgiving deity. In Islam there is no personal god (no heavenly Father and no personal Saviour). Some of the differences between the religions are set out in the book entitled *The Empty Promise of Godism* which is available for free download on the Glory to Glory website – see especially chapter 6.

Forgiveness of sins is essential in order for there to be fellowship with God – Father, Son and Holy Spirit (see especially 1 John **1**:3 and 2 Corinthians **13**:14.) The apostle Paul's frequently-used phrase 'in Christ' and 'in the Lord' (164 times) signifies a profound communion with God, and refers to people whose sins have been forgiven. Forgiveness is at the heart of the Christian life and message.

10

THE NEW BIRTH

Background

The new birth is an absolute necessity for salvation. Jesus said, "*I tell you the truth, unless one is born again, he cannot see the kingdom of God*" (John **3**:3). Being born again involves a change of heart and life. There is real trust in Jesus' having paid the penalty for my sin, believing on him as my only Saviour; there is surrender of my life to Jesus, accepting his 'lordship' (he is in charge of my life from now on!) I am now truly his *disciple*, beginning on 'the Way'. The *new life* as a faithful and true believer and follower of Jesus now *begins*. The theological word 'regeneration' is used for this event. A child cannot conceive itself and humans cannot regenerate themselves! The Spirit of God is at work. A person who repents before God and believes in and receives Jesus as Lord and Saviour is 'born of God'. (See John **1**:13). It is a turning point; indeed it could be said to be the person's second birthday!

A New Relationship

A new relationship with God through Jesus Christ has now begun, and one result of this is a new outlook on life. The old outlook was marred and marked by sin, even if a person had previously been in some sense 'trying to lead a good life' in their own strength. There is real moral change, and this can often be very noticeable to the new believer and to others. The new birth implies newness of life in Christ Jesus – and this process is brought about by the gracious act (gift) of God (see Ephesians **2**:8–9).

An unregenerate person is blind to the things of God. In fact the 'problem' is not so much that we cannot 'see' the things of God, it is much more serious than that. We are spiritually dead and need to be born again, and until we are born again we remain dead in our sins. Jesus came to restore sight to the blind (Luke **4**:18–21) and this has an extra layer of meaning in this context: spiritual blindness would be dealt with, as well as physical blindness. Sin must be dealt with by repentance and the forgiveness won by Jesus on the cross; the old evil nature is then disarmed. (See Psalm **51**:5; Jeremiah **17**:9; Mark **7**:21–23; John **3**:3–6; Romans **6**:6 and **8**:7–8; 1 Corinthians **2**:14; Ephesians **2**:3.)

The decision to follow Jesus, as Lord and as Saviour (and to recognise him as Messiah – the Saviour sent by the Father) is a serious one and is an act of faith. After repentance and trusting in the blood of Jesus, a spiritual new birth follows which it is impossible for humans to describe adequately. A child of God has been given new birth, '…into a living hope through the resurrection… into an inheritance that can never perish, spoil, or fade (see 1 Peter **1**:3–4; and note that there is also a future dimension: a 'salvation that is ready to be revealed', mentioned in v. 5).

The concept of 'sonship' here is applicable whether we are male or female – because in biblical times its meaning included inheritance. Sonship (by adoption and grace) is given once only to the new believer. Sadly, disciples of Jesus who have been born again can and do sin, and the New Testament recognises this and helps us to deal with it (see, for example, 1 John **1**:8–9). There is still a battle between the 'born again' believer and the world, the flesh and the devil. But the regenerate Christian is now aware of the battle in a new way, and knows that the Lord is with him to help him to resist evil and overcome the assaults of the enemy. After any 'backsliding' or known sin, a disciple of Jesus must seek forgiveness – but this does not mean being born again a second or third time.[1]

See Matthew **18**:3; John **1**:12–13; **3**:14–15; **5**:24; Acts **3**:19; **4**:10; **16**:30–31; Galatians **3**:24–26.

Like any new born, a child of God will grow and mature as time goes by. 'Sanctification' is a process which continues throughout the rest of the believer's life. There should be a progressive change, as a disciple becomes more like Christ. Have you made that first step of repentance and faith in Jesus Christ? When you have been born again, you know at the deepest level that, by the cross and resurrection of Jesus you were saved from the *penalty* of past sin. (See the note below on the other 'tenses' of salvation. See the separate study No. 13 on Assurance. See also 2 Corinthians **5**:17; Ephesians **2**:10 and **4**:24; Galatians **2**:20 and **6**:15; Colossians **3**:1–10; 1 Peter **1**:22–23; 2 Peter **1**:4; 1 John **5**:11–12.)

[1] Note

Some have claimed that final apostasy is not possible for true disciples of Jesus. But there are many passages in the New Testament which indicate otherwise. Consider that Jesus' teaching on hell was given in the Gospels to believers. Consider Jesus' warning concerning those who will be unready for his Second Coming (see Matthew chapters **24** and **25**). Consider the fate of Judas Iscariot. Consider Paul's many warnings as to the need for perseverance. See also Hebrews **12**:25. The believer is to be one who overcomes, not walking in sin and disobedience. (See Revelation **21**:7–8). All Christians should prayerfully seek to understand the issues at stake here as they are extremely serious. From the New Testament we learn about having been saved from the penalty of past sin (which is one thing that happens when we repent, believe, and are born again), and of *being saved* from the power of sin (note the continuous present tense; we need to go on fighting the good fight against sin, and we have the help of the Holy Spirit in that fight); and of a future hope of being with Christ in a place where there is no presence of sin. So 'being saved' does not mean the same as 'safe'. To *begin* a new life is not the same thing as living it out faithfully and walking in obedience. The following book is recommended as a helpful study of the relevant biblical teaching: *Once Saved, Always Saved?* by David Pawson (published by Hodder).

11

GRACE

What does the Bible mean by grace?

Basically, it is God's favour shown to humans, and is rightly termed 'unmerited favour' for we have not earned it in any way. The term is most widely understood in connection with God's grace given to those people who put their trust in Jesus as Lord and Saviour. The full expression of that grace is in the salvation of those who truly believe. It has been said that under law God demands righteousness from all people and under grace God gives righteousness to those who believe. It is by God's grace that we may be saved, and not by any righteousness of our own. It is by grace, and only by grace, that we may be saved. (See Ephesians **2**:1–9.)

The era of grace began in the world with the death and resurrection of Christ Jesus

Titus **3**:4–5; John **1**:17; **1**:12–13, **3**:36; Romans **3**:24–27; **5**:2; 15–21; **6**:14; 2 Corinthians **6**:1–3; **8**:9; Galatians **1**:3–15; **2**:21; **5**:4

The law (Heb. *Torah*) makes God's righteous demands. The Ten Commandments (see Exodus **20**), and our Lord's summary of the law (Matthew **22**:37–40) are of special significance.

Grace is God's gift to enable mankind to live holy lives

It might be said, then, that: *law demands – grace gives*.

Deuteronomy **5**:6–22; 1 John **4**:19–**5**:21 (speaks of the love of God in giving Jesus, His Son); John **1**:12, **3**:16; Romans **3**:21–24, **8**:3, **10**:4–10; Philippians **3**:9, **4**:13; Hebrews **7**:19; Psalm **51**:11–17; Ephesians **5**:15–20

In life we can either live under law, or under grace

This is the fundamental choice before all people, whether they acknowledge it, or not. The biblical record shows clearly that under law, before the time of Christ, mankind as a whole failed, and ended by crucifying Jesus. Similarly, the era of grace will also end in the failure of mankind – this time evidenced most clearly in its final persecution of Jewish people and believing Jews and Christians. This will be a time of a turning away from truth – even by some within the church. But it is mankind that fails – not God's plan of grace.

2 Corinthians **4**:3 – 4; 2 Timothy **3**:1–8; 1 John **4**:1–3; 2 Peter **2**:1; Jude 4, 8, 11–13, 16

The simplicity and freedom of grace is God's final plan of salvation for the world

Any other 'gospel' is an anathema to God. Acts **4**:12; Romans **10**:9 – 13 (see also Ezekiel **34**); Galatians **1**:8 – 9; John **10**:1–21

Common Grace

There is a second concept of grace – the idea of common grace. Put simply, common grace is God's loving and favourable attitude to humans *per se*, being demonstrated in all those blessings that stop short of actual salvation. The key text that illustrates this is Matthew **5**:44–5: *". . . Love your enemies and pray for those who persecute you, so that you may be sons of your father who is in heaven. For he makes the sun to rise on the evil and the good, and sends rain on the just and on the unjust . . . ."*

Many things that life has to offer may be enjoyed by and available to even those who refuse to believe. Health, friendships, successes and human love are generally available to all mankind to greater or lesser degree. The fact that so many fail to enjoy these things seems to be at least partly because of the sinful and fallen world in which we live. Passages that underline this idea of *common grace* are: Psalm **36**:5–7; Psalm **145**:9, 14–17; Acts **14**:15–17; Acts **17**:24–28. These passages testify to the good will of God towards all humanity. When we sin and suffer for our sins, this is in spite of God's goodness, and in spite of his gift of grace through Jesus. We emphasise, however, that the key understanding of grace is in relation to what Jesus has done on the cross.

12

ETERNAL LIFE

Background: what *is* eternal life?

In ancient Greek thought the concept of 'immortality of the soul' for humans was significant. But the biblical expression 'eternal life' signifies far more than immortality. It is certainly clear from the Bible that we all survive death, and a vital question for everyone is: will this state be *eternal life* or conscious separation from God for ever?

Scholars debate the word 'eternal'. Some emphasise that it is a word of *duration*, and others *quality*. When you think of duration it is translated 'everlasting' —meaning life that goes on forever. But others point out that eternal life means life of a good quality, signifying life worth living, everlasting and abundant; life *in* Jesus who is himself the life.

When do we begin to experience eternal life?

On being born-again (see Study No. 10) we begin knowing the new quality of life 'in Christ' which is called 'eternal life'. God is eternal. He is the I AM, the eternal one. Eternal life was experienced by humans at the beginning, but because of Adam's rebellion (Genesis chapter 3, recounting the Fall) and the consequent separation of man from God, eternal life became possible only on God's post-Fall terms. (See Exodus **3**:14; Matthew **25**:46; John **1**:1–4; **3**:3–20, 36; **5**:24-27, 39-40; **6**:27; **6**:68; **8**:12; **10**:10; **11**:25; **12**:25; **20**:31; 1 Timothy **6**:12; Titus **1**:2; 1 John **1**:1–2; Revelation **1**:8, 18; **22**:13.)

Can we lose eternal life?[1]

We have noted that we begin to enjoy eternal life when we are *in Christ*. In John chapter 3 it is clear from the Greek continuous present tense used that we must *go on believing* in order to *go on having* eternal life. So it is clearly possible to 'walk away from' eternal life – in other words to come under condemnation again (see again Study No. 10 and the 'Final thoughts' section of that study). You may encounter a range of views on this matter. The debate has centred on the claim by some preachers that believers are 'once saved, always saved' (an expression which is absent from the Bible). Jesus told disciples about the vital importance of *abiding* in him. Disciples are to persevere in a walk of obedience, and not fall away.

Faithful discipleship

Our experience of eternal life begins as we become a *new creation*. We *repent* and *believe* in Jesus as our Lord and Saviour and are *baptised in water and Spirit*. The new nature we are given will result in a radical new life and vitality as we go on being filled with the Spirit – but there will be struggles to overcome with his help. The names of believers (i.e. Jesus' *faithful* disciples – and that is all who go on faithfully believing in him, putting their trust and allegiance in him, walking in obedience) are written in the Book of Life. (See Romans **6**:4, 22–23; **8**:2, 6, 10; 2 Corinthians **4**:10; **5**:17; Galatians **2**:20; **6**:8; Ephesians **4**:17-28; Philippians **2**:16; James **1**:12; 1 John **3**:14–15; **5**:12–13; Revelation **3**:5; **13**:8; **17**:8; **20**:11-15. See also Genesis **3**:22–24 and Revelation **2**:7.)

[1] **Note**

To clarify, see the following extract from *Is John 3:16 the Gospel?* by David Pawson, pp. 85-86 (© Used by permission, Terra Nova Publications; book & ebook available). Note the author's translation from the Greek original (in 2nd paragraph):

ETERNAL LIFE

. . . Perhaps one of the most common misconceptions is that eternal life is a package that has been transferred to us when we believed in Jesus so that *we now have this package*, we now have eternal life . . . and we have got it for ever. The notion that you can *lose* eternal life is very new to many, many Christians, because the majority . . . have been told that you cannot, and that once you have got eternal life you have got it eternally, and that is settled for ever . . . . So often we are reading John 3:16 with a prejudiced mind, a mind that says 'once believe, always believe', or 'once saved, always saved'. So we read the tenses differently. Instead of realising it says '*God once loved . . .*', and, '*If we go on believing, we go on having life*', we switch the tenses back to front, and say, 'God goes on loving, and we only need to believe once.' So we have reversed the message because we have been reading it through certain spectacles. The message of John 3:16 (read as carefully as possible) is that eternal life can be lost, and you can cease to be having eternal life by ceasing to believe in him who died for us . . . .

. . . *God has given us eternal life, and this life is in his Son. He who is having the Son is having life and he who is not having the Son is not having life* (1 John 5:12). 'Having' is in the present continuous tense. The key there is that God has given us eternal life but this life is not in us. This life is in his Son; we are only given that life in his Son. We are not given it in ourselves. Therefore, as John goes on to say, *he who is having the Son*, or literally, *he who goes on having the Son*, goes on having life. But he who *does not go on having the Son* does not go on having life. Eternal life is not in the Christian, it is in Christ.

13
ASSURANCE

Background

Consider for a moment how those who know Jesus as their personal Lord and Saviour may appear to others. Unbelievers can find it hard to understand how it is that Bible-believing Christians seem to have a deep, abiding *confidence* which marks their *belief* in Jesus and *relationship* with him. How can it be that so many of his followers are so convinced? Clearly this is more than intellectual certitude – that is part of it, but it is clearly *relational* too. There is evidently something going on here which is about *knowing a person* as well as being able to say what is true of that person; and both kinds of 'knowing' have important consequences for everything in the believer's life in all its aspects – including what they say and how they behave. This often shows itself in the ethical area; it will certainly be obvious in the Christian believer's abhorrence of the worship of other gods.

The profound awareness of a relationship which the believer experiences – and which can survive all challenges, obstacles, tests and trials in this world – is attested throughout the New Testament. The Epistle to the Hebrews speaks about the 'hope of which we boast' (**3**:6; see also **6**:11; and see **6**:19, from which we learn that the hope believers have is an 'anchor for the soul'), and the assurance of faith (Hebrews **10**:22; see also **11**:1).

What do we really mean by 'assurance' in this context?

The believer's firm underlying conviction is that by faith he or she is '*in Christ*' – having *been saved* from the *penalty* of past sins by the grace of God, through faith in Jesus Christ and his one sacrifice of himself on the cross; that the believer is now *being saved* through the work of the Holy Spirit in our sanctification (with which we are to co-operate) from the *power* of sin; and, looking forward to the great salvation which is to come, that the believer will ultimately know salvation from the *presence* of sin, when Christ will have judged the living and the dead. To be living *in him*, walking in faithful obedience, led by the Holy Spirit, means that one is being *kept* in eternal life which is found only *in* Christ. Thus we are to *abide* in him and to *go on believing in Jesus*.

That living faith is the essential reality underlying Christian assurance. We can have assurance because of the promises given by Jesus.

John **3**:1-21; **4**:13-14; **8**:12; **10**:7-10.

If we fall away, if we stop believing in Jesus, we may lose that true assurance. The answer to that is to return to him in repentance (remembering, of course, the great truth that to 'repent' means not merely feeling sorry – it includes stopping doing whatever it is that is offensive to God).

What about false 'assurance'

There can be a false sense of 'assurance', of course. The Bible does not license persistent, unrepented, ungodly, sinful behaviour. Those who may once have believed in Jesus, who perhaps went forward at an evangelistic rally, but then fell away into grave sin and unbelief, are deluding themselves (and, sadly, maybe others too, if they reach positions of leadership) if they imagine that their final salvation is assured no matter what they later believe or do. The Epistle of Jude and the Book of Revelation make that perfectly clear. See Studies 10 and 12 in this series – students may want to refer to these for a balanced view on this vital subject. It is important to know that when we are continuing faithfully believing and trusting in Jesus, and are being led by the Holy Spirit, and are walking in obedience and repenting as and when the Spirit shows us to do so, we are being 'kept', and we are not going to be snatched out of Jesus' hand by some external force against our will.

Galatians **6**:7-10; 1 John **5**:1-10

Is this a matter of 'feelings'?

We are human, and of course we have feelings, but the kind of assurance attested to in the Epistle to the Hebrews means something much more than just the way we feel! Assurance can only be known in real, living faith; in belief and personal trust in God – the true God, the God of Abraham, Isaac and Jacob, the Father of our Lord Jesus Christ. We know he keeps his word. We trust his promises. We know and trust in Jesus Christ for he is our Lord: he has 'lordship' over you as a Christian – he is in charge, he has authority over you and you seek to obey him. That is a very practical, day-to-day fact about the Christian life. So assurance does not depend on our own feelings, which can change. Real assurance provides inner, personal confidence in our God.

1 John **4**:7-21

What if I lack assurance? How can it be obtained?

As indicated already, we are to have faith in God's word (John **5**:24).

Jesus always *spoke* the truth. So begin by reading again the things that he taught, as recorded in the four Gospels. *Every word he uttered was truth and utterly dependable*. Look at the context of his words and ask: was he speaking to believers? He mainly spoke to Jews and could take for granted that they knew basic truths about God's self-revelation in what we call the Old Testament. God had been revealing himself to his people for many generations before he sent his Son, the Messiah (anointed one).

Remember that Jesus himself *is* the truth. He said so, and the New Testament testifies to this. He is the eternal *word* (Greek: *logos*; see John **1**:1). This means much more than the words we use in our human languages. It is a term of profound significance, and it signifies here the second person of the Holy Trinity. Jesus is perfect man and he is God incarnate.

Witnessing to Jesus, the Messiah – letting others know the essential truth that he is Lord, in charge of our lives, and that every knee will bow to him, and that he was raised from the dead and lives now – is vital. This has to do with our salvation (see Romans **10**:9–11). Of course we need to have assurance first, to know that we belong to him – or we can scarcely witness to others. But as we have courage to bear witness, our confidence grows. Testimony to the reality of the work of the Lord our God is a blessing to those who hear. The assurance of victory comes from a clear conscience. The believer is to walk in the way of obedience to God. So there is to be no known, unconfessed sin or stiff-necked attitude marring our relationship with God.

We should be wary of false assurance based on self-effort, men's praise or 'success'.

Psalm **17**:8; **91**:11; **121**:3, 8; Isaiah **26**:3; Matthew **7**:22–23 (false assurance); John **10**:10–14, 27–30; **11**:26; **17**:11; Romans **8**:28–39; 2 Corinthians **1**:10; Ephesians **1**:13; **4**:30; Philippians **1**:3–6; Titus **1**:1–3; Hebrews **6**:11; **7**:25; **10**:19–23; Jude v. 24; Revelation **3**:10.

Summary

There are two main aspects to assurance:

(1) There is an immediate assurance that is the gift of every person who is born again.

(2) There is an ongoing and developing assurance as we live out our lives in the care of Jesus, our Saviour, following him in his Way as his disciples.

In the second aspect we will see victory over doubt and temptation, and we will see answers to prayer. Life will not necessarily be easy and our discipleship may be imperfect, but nevertheless we see God's hand at work and our assurance is confirmed as we grow and mature.

Isaiah **32**:17 [RSV] (Peace, quietness and trust); Romans **8**:15–16, 38–39; 2 Timothy **1**:12; **3**:14–17; **4**:8, 18; 1 Peter **1**:3-9; Jude v. 1.

Note

Whilst some of the Old Testament references are made in relation to Israel, God's chosen people, they nevertheless show God's heart towards all those whom he has chosen and who follow him faithfully. We can justifiably assert that they apply to the faithful followers of Jesus, the Jewish Messiah.

14
DEATH – PHYSICAL

Background

With the exception of those who are alive at the time when Jesus returns, we must all die at some time. Physical death is not the same as spiritual death (see Study No. 15). Spiritual death means eternal, conscious separation from God. Although physical death is that of the body, the soul lives on. For this universal effect, there must be a universal cause. We learn from the Bible that sin entered the world through one man (Adam), and death through sin. (See Romans 5:12–14.) Whilst the rebellion of Adam can be accepted as an actual event in time, we can also affirm with clarity that all individual men and women rebel (sin) against God and so what the Bible says is true – the wages of sin is death.

Genesis **2**:17; Ezekiel **18**:1–32; Romans **6**:16, 23; **8**:6, 13; 1 Corinthians **15**:21–22.

Physical pain and death were not what God originally intended for his creation. Longevity was a feature of early mankind. Universal death (physical corruption) accompanies universal moral corruption.

Psalm **14**:1–3; Jeremiah **17**:9; Mark **7**:21–23; 1 Corinthians **15**:22; 2 Corinthians **5**:4; Galatians **5**:19–24; 1 Peter **1**:22–25.

What does Jesus teach about death?

Jesus' life was touched by bereavement if we may assume that Joseph died some time before Jesus began his earthly ministry. Jesus wept in Bethany at the death of his friend Lazarus (John **11**:35), and he spoke about life after death,

65

and about judgement, heaven and hell. After death there will be a separation of the righteous and the wicked. The gospel message brought the good news of peace with God through righteousness – ultimately through the righteousness of Jesus himself. His teaching indicated the reality of eternal life or eternal punishment – see, for example, the parable of a man named Lazarus (not to be confused with the Lazarus who was raised by Jesus in Bethany; Luke **16**:19–31). In the parable, Jesus speaks of Hades – the world of the dead, understood to be the place where unrepentant sinners reside until the final day of judgement. Remember that we learn what we know about hell from the lips of Jesus himself. We know that believers should fear God, who has the power to throw them into hell. (See Luke **12**:4–5; an aspect of revealed truth which is not much emphasised by many preachers today.)

Jesus recognised the reality of death, and he knew that he himself would suffer and be put to death.

Jesus conquered death

Jesus, who for our sakes submitted to physical death, conquered death. He was raised from the dead, victorious, on the third day. His tomb was left empty. For the saved man or woman, death has to be gone through, but it should hold no horrors for believers walking in obedience because, like the apostle Paul, we long to see our Lord (Philippians **1**:23). But death and what lies beyond it remain the ultimate horror for those who die in their sins, rejecting the cross of Christ.

John **20**:3–9; Acts **2**:24; 1 Thessalonians **4**:13–18

God is the God of the living. It is made abundantly clear in the teaching of Jesus in the Gospels, and in the Book of Revelation, that after death will come judgement: the Lord Jesus Christ will return to judge the living and the dead. He will judge with justice. It will be crucial that we shall die believing and trusting in him, as faithful overcomers. But it may be asked: what happens to the souls of the deceased between their death and the day of judgement when the secrets of all hearts will be revealed? The New Testament uses the picture of 'sleep' to describe the state of the dead who are awaiting the Lord's return. (See 1 Thessalonians **4**:13–**5**:11 to learn more about this revealed truth and its significance for how we should be living our lives here and now). Our minds turn to the promise of Jesus to the thief on the cross next to him (see Luke **23**:39–43). Was that a special case or a more general indication of the state all faithful, repentant, God-fearing believers will experience after death? Scripture does not answer all our questions, and we have to allow for the fact that time itself may be rather different in the world to come. Are we conscious of the passage of time when we are asleep? That seemingly hard question is answered for us if we will meditate on what the Lord has revealed about how time is in his sight:

> Before the mountains were born or you brought forth the whole world, from everlasting to everlasting you are God . . . . a thousand years in your sight are like a day that has just gone by, or like a watch in the night.
>
> Psalm **90**:2, 4, NIV

The false doctrine of purgatory must be rejected – it appears to have arisen through misinterpretation of 1 Corinthians **3**:15. Historically, certain practices associated with prayer for the dead may have brought some material wealth to religion which taught that false doctrine, but we must hold fast to Jesus' teaching. There is an unbridgeable divide between the saved and the unsaved, at the point of death.

Luke **16**:23, 26; Luke **20**:37–38; John **5**:24; Hebrews **9**:27; 1 John **1**:7; Revelation **21**:6-7.

15
DEATH – SPIRITUAL

Background

We have considered (in Unit 14) physical death, which we all know about – it happens to us all and is a publicly observed and recorded event. Spiritual death is harder for most people to understand, mainly because they are unaware that there is anything dead about them: we think we are fully alive already. Yet we learn from the teaching of Jesus that in our natural, sinful state, there is something at the heart of who we are which is *dead*, and that we therefore need to be made alive by the work of the Holy Spirit. We need to be 'born again'; we need to move from death to real life, and only God will be able to change us so radically that we are truly living. The heart of what we are needs to be changed.

John **3**:1-21; **5**:24-25; **9**:39

Death a result of the Fall

This has to be our starting point. It crops up time and again in these studies, because it explains our condition and our need. When mankind first sinned against the Creator, death came in. (See Genesis chapter **3**, and Paul's clear explanation in Romans **5**:12-14.) It has continuing effects and remains a battle (see Romans **6**:16). We can never recover from spiritual death by our own attempts to change ourselves (in our own strength).

Life

We all know that we cannot give ourselves life. Life, including true spiritual life, is from God. It is found *in* Christ, but apart from Christ there is a terrible spiritual deadness. That is why we see mankind in its present state. (See Romans **8**:1-11.)

Prophets

The classical prophets of the Old Testament were aware and affirmed that spiritual life was known to the righteous, those walking in practical faith and obedience to God. See, for example, Ezekiel **18**:1-9; and in the rest of that chapter the ways of life and death are described. In Joel chapter **2** the promise of an outpouring of the Spirit is given (which was to be fulfilled at Pentecost; see Acts chapter **2**).

New Testament

Hebrew thought considered a person as a unity (see Genesis **2**:7; man became a living being when God breathed life into him). However, mind [Greek: *psuche*] and spirit [*pneuma*] are referred to in Scripture, as well as body [*soma*]. How these distinctions operate and what is signified by each is too large a study to embark upon here.[1] Scholars are divided as to whether 'soul' and the human 'spirit' are best described as distinct or as essentially signifying the non-physical aspect of a human being by both terms. When Jesus said, *"Rather, be afraid of the One who can destroy both soul and body in hell"* (see Matthew **10**:28), we see that the soul must survive death to be in that terrible state (as well as there being a 'body'). Different books of the New Testament allow for some interchangeability of terms. Thus in the Epistle to the Hebrews, those who have died are sometimes called 'spirits' (Hebrews **12**:23), and in 1 Peter **3**:19, we read of *spirits* in prison. And in Revelation **6**:9 and **20**:4 we have references to the 'souls' of martyred believers.

However we understand the relation between the biblical

usage of the two terms, what is perfectly clear is that the 'born again', Spirit-filled believer who is walking in obedience is experiencing eternal life (see Unit 12). We are aware of having passed from death to life (Jesus warned his own disciples of the risk of destruction in hell; and elsewhere in the NT there are warnings about falling away, failing to 'abide in' Jesus Christ – and falling back into sinful behaviour or apostasy [see Jude and Hebrews]). So spiritual death appears to remain a terrible possibility for a former believer who has abandoned his faith, rejects Christ and finally refuses to repent.

From Scripture it is clear that spiritual death entails eternal separation from God and torment, with consequent pain, sorrow, anguish and fire.

Yet the believer can always hold on to the great affirmations of hope for faithful believers in Jesus Christ. The New Testament has a great many such words of encouragement and promise.

The terrible truth about spiritual death

We have to be aware that it was Jesus himself who spelt out the consequences of what we call 'eternal death'. One writer explains some of the New Testament teaching on hell in this way:

It is a place of spiritual death. It is called 'the second death'. Death is separation. Hell is separation from God. It is 'outside'. There will be no worship there, for there will be no God to worship. Prayer will be equally futile. When all contact with the divine has been lost, the human also disappears. The image of God is totally defaced. Personal disintegration inevitably follows.

The absence of God is matched in horror by the presence of Satan, the source of all evil. Thousands of his 'angels' (since their rebellion against heaven, they are known as 'demons') will swell the population, polluting the atmosphere with their foul thoughts, words and deeds. The absence of every virtue will be matched by the presence of every vice. No wonder Jesus addressed those condemned to such company as 'you who are cursed' (Matthew **25**:41).

In both the gospels and Revelation, the word 'torment' (*basanismos* and its cognates) occurs quite frequently. Akin to 'torture', it signifies conscious pain, whether physical or mental....[2]

There is much more that could be said on this subject, and it is sobering to reflect that the heart of the New Testament teaching concerning hell is directly from the lips of Jesus speaking to disciples. The fear of God is indeed still the beginning of wisdom for disciples of Jesus Christ.

Matthew **8**:22; **13**:42, 49-50; **25**:46; Luke **13**:24-27; **15**:24; Romans **5**:12; **6**:16, 23; **8**:13, 16; 1 Corinthians **15**:21-22; 2 Corinthians **6**:2; Ephesians **2**:1-3; **4**:17-18; Colossians **2**:13; 1 John **5**:12; Revelation **2**:11; **20**:6, 10, 14-15; **21**:8

Notes

[1] An excellent biblical study of the topic is provided in *Systematic Theology* by Wayne Grudem (IVP and Zondervan, 1994) p.472ff.

[2] *The Road to Hell*, David Pawson (©Terra Nova Publications, 2007).

16
SEPARATION

Background

The thread of redemption throughout the Bible demonstrates God's will to be that man should be able to have a relationship of love and trust towards him, expressed in obedience. Since the time when Adam and Eve were driven from the Garden for disobedience, God has patiently sought to restore their (our) lost relationship through the witness of people of faith. Faithful obedience was demonstrated by Noah, and God gave a great covenant promise when he saved him from a wicked generation. Abraham was a great man of faith, obedient to God, and God gave the great 'Abrahamic' covenant through him. God gave a covenant to the Hebrew people through Moses, to whom he gave the law (*Torah*) at Mount Sinai. (See Exodus **25**:8; **29**:45–46; Psalm **107**.) Finally, the great messianic covenant was sealed by the blood of Jesus, who spoke to his disciples at the Last Supper of the new covenant. (See Note 1.) God had repeatedly rescued his people when they cried out to him. Finally, as recorded in the New Testament, Jesus Christ, the only-begotten Son of God, true God and true man, came to earth as the Messiah. He came to save people from their sin, and to provide the means to fulfil the divine plan of redemption.

God is perfectly good, holy, righteous and just, and our sin causes a barrier, separating us from him. Our transgressions (whether stemming from ignorance or from deliberately wilful disobedience to his perfect law), our selfishness, our rebellion and the replacement of him at the centre of our lives by other things, all these separate us from him, and must ultimately be punished, for a holy God cannot dwell with sin. (See Isaiah **59**:2; Ezekiel **14**:7; Hosea **9**:10.) It is only by his grace, through faith in the finished saving work of Jesus, who took the full punishment for our sins on the cross, that we can approach him, and make a sanctuary where he may dwell.

Types of separation in Scripture
- separation of physical things (Genesis 1:4 – light from darkness)
- separation from God because of sin (Isaiah 59:2)
- separation of individuals to God for ministry (Aaron – 1 Chronicles 23:13)
- separation of chosen groups for ministry (Levites – Deuteronomy 10:8)
- separation of the Hebrew nation for witness (Israel – Exodus 33:16; Leviticus 20:24; 1 Kings 8:53)
- separation of nations (ethnic groups) for judgment (Matthew 25:32)
- separation of people for the work of the gospel (Paul – Romans 1:1)
- separation of the righteous from rebellious people (Numbers 16:21; Ezra 6:21; Luke 6:22)
- separation of righteous from the wicked (ultimate – Matthew 13:49)
- separation from impurity and uncleanness (2 Corinthians 6:17)
- separation from the world (sanctification of believers by the word of truth – John 17:14–16; renewing of the mind – Romans 12:2)

As Jesus prayed to the Father, he declared of believers that, *"They are not of the world...."*

The desire for worldly pleasures as ends in themselves is sinful. [This is not about the proper appreciation of God's good gifts in creation; we give thanks to him for those gifts. He gives them for proper use in accordance with his purposes and law. What is forbidden is greed, envy, covetousness, improper usages forbidden in God's law, and placing created things above the Creator (a form of idolatry)].

For mankind, therefore, separation is thus usually *from* evil people, sinful actions and attitudes, though we are still 'in the world' and are to witness in the midst of human life, and there may be separation *for* God for a holy work. We are to be consecrated in a process of sanctification, believers trusting in him and obeying him, living in faith (which includes faithfulness). (See Exodus **33**:16; Leviticus **15**:31; 1 Chronicles **23**:13; John **17**:14–16.) To be an effective and true disciple of Jesus inevitably must involve a measure of separation from worldly things.

Compromise

To attack the purpose and value of separation from evil or separation to the Lord, Satan offers compromise, usually in a subtle and disguised form. Consider Pharaoh's offers (in a sequence of deception) to Moses, who sought to obey God's command to lead the Hebrew people out of Egypt to worship God. Pharaoh says to Moses, and by implication to us:

Exodus **8**:25. Do your religious practices where you are (in Egypt – in sin). The suggestion is: it is fine here – don't stand out, stay in prison under our yoke, you don't need to leave.

Exodus **8**:28. Go a little way, but not too far. The enemy's suggestion, and the temptation for us, would be: do not be disciplined for the Lord, don't be zealous, then it won't cost you so much. (But see Luke **14**:26–27.)

Exodus **10**:11. The wrong suggestion here is: go with only some of your people; don't care for your family, or your other responsibilities.

Exodus **10**:24. The temptation is to leave parts of life (including means of livelihood) out of the matter. But God wants the whole of us, not just part!

Satan's offer of compromise can be like this: 'Don't overdo it! Partial obedience is OK, little white lies don't count, keep the best for yourself.' But Moses was strong – 'No hoof shall be left behind'. There can be no compromise with sin if we want to know God's presence. Separation from the world requires clean, deliberate godly choices to be made. Lot's wife looked back at Sodom (Genesis **19**:26) and died as a result. Compromise always involves mixed lifestyles, and that can set a person on the broad way which leads to ruin.

Moses chose to suffer affliction rather than enjoy the pleasures of sin for a short time. (See Exodus **10**:26.)

Jesus was always faithful and obedient to the Father. His example encourages us to make a good choice into a habit, and a good habit into a permanent feature of our character.

1 Corinthians **10**:20; Hebrews **5**:8 and **11**:25; Revelation **22**:11.

Choices

Jesus chooses his disciples out of the world, and Paul instructs them to purge out the sin-life, even if it means separation from worldly or disorderly 'friends', and from uncleanness and youthful lusts.

God invites us to draw near to him. He provides the only way, the new and living way – for which the believer has been cleansed by the blood of Jesus. Make a choice today to separate yourself from the world's attractions and temptations, and separate yourself from them for the living God. Draw near to him. If we seek him, and search for him with all our heart, his promise is that he will be found by us.

Psalm **65**:4; Psalm **73**:28a; Jeremiah **29**:13–14; John **15**:18–19 and **17**:6, 14–17; 1 Corinthians **5**:7; 1 Thessalonians **4**:7; 1 Timothy **3**:14–15; 2 Timothy **2**:22; Hebrews **10**:19–22.

Note

Two useful books available from Glory to Glory Publications look at the subject of the covenants: *Defending Christian Zionism*, David Pawson; *The Case for Enlargement Theology*, Alex Jacob.

17
SANCTIFICATION

Background

Sanctification has been called the highway to holiness. It is God's will for those people who are chosen for salvation through the sanctifying work of the Holy Spirit and belief in the truth of God's Word. He desires that we are cleansed for fellowship with him through redemption by the sprinkling of the blood of Jesus. (See 1 Thessalonians **4**:3; 2 Thessalonians **2**:13; 1 Peter **1**:2.)

Sanctification means the process of being made holy (or saintly). There are two aspects to this process – being separated from sin (and from the world's way of thinking and doing), and also being separated to God's way of living. The first reference to sanctification in the Old Testament concerns the Sabbath (the seventh day, *Shabbat*), which God blessed and sanctified. This day was to be set apart from other days for rest, and consecrated to God. (See Genesis **2**:3; Deuteronomy **5**:12; Nehemiah **13**:22.)

There are many things and tasks that God required to be sanctified under the Mosaic covenant. Everything used for his service was to be made holy. This included: the tabernacle or temple (where he was present in a special way), the people, the priests; also a man's house or field, his first-born, his offerings to the Lord, and everything used to make atonement for sin (all the vessels of the tabernacle or temple). God (and his Name) was to be sanctified (held as holy) in the eyes of the people, through righteousness, through his bringing of his people back to their Land, through his judgment of the nations, and through the keeping of

Shabbat as holy to him. (See Exodus **13**:2; **19**:10; **28**:41; **29**:27; **29**:43; **30**:26-29; **31**:13-14; Leviticus **27**:14,17; Isaiah **5**:16; Ezekiel **20**:41; **28**:22; **36**:23; Joel **1**:14; 1 Corinthians **6**:19.)

Many times in his Word, God says to his people, *sanctify yourselves*. Mostly this is in preparation for some future action: for judgment, for miracles, for making sacrifice to the Lord, or for touching holy things, and God castigates the people for insufficient or false sanctification. (See Joshua **3**:5; **7**:13, 1 Samuel **16**:5; 1 Chronicles **15**:12; 2 Chronicles **30**:3; **35**:6; Isaiah **66**:17.)

The Process of Sanctification

There are two processes involved – cleansing and sanctifying. In Ephesians **5**:25-27, Paul tells us that Jesus loved his church so that he might sanctify and cleanse it. To be sanctified, one must be made clean and pure. Jesus' redemption of the church cleanses and sanctifies, in order that he might present it without spot or wrinkle, holy and without blemish. That has both personal and corporate aspects. (See Matthew **16**:8.)

To his disciples, Jesus says: *You are already clean because of the Word I have spoken to you.* And for those who sin, John says that if we walk in the light and confess our sins, the blood of Jesus cleanses us from all sin and unrighteousness. Both 'water' and the blood of Jesus are required for sanctification. Man needs both redemption through the shed blood of Jesus, and inward washing by his Word. The Old Testament sacrifices for sin (with the combination of the shedding of blood upon the altar, and the washing in the laver) speak to us both of Jesus' shed blood on the cross and the continual inward washing that we need through the truth of his Word. (See John **15**:3; 1 John **1**:7, 9; 1 John **5**:6; Hebrews **9**:14, **13**:12.)

In scripture we learn of a number of ways in which God's people have been sanctified. In the Mosaic covenant it was the offering of sacrifices on a physical altar. In the new (Messianic) covenant we think of: the Holy Spirit; the truth of the Word of God; Jesus himself, crucified once for us and risen from the dead; and our belief and faith in the Lord Jesus. (See Matthew **23**:19; John **17**:17; Acts **26**:18; 2 Thessalonians **2**:13; Hebrews **10**:29; 1 Peter **1**:2.)

Separation from sin is thus a vital stage in the process of sanctification, that we might be enabled by God to be in relationship with himself, the one who is perfectly holy. Romans **12**:1-2 shows us the changes that are needed in this process. We present our bodies as a living sacrifice to God, as on an altar, holy and acceptable. We are not conformed to worldly values, but transformed by renewal of our minds (our way of thinking) by his Spirit, so that we can know God's will for us and embrace his inward washing by the truth of his Word. This leads to a new way of living, so that we can think and do as Jesus would have us think and do. Paul encourages us to be spiritually discerning; and have 'the mind of Christ' (1 Corinthians **2**:16). True sanctification goes beyond 'Do not look, Do not touch, Do not taste, Do not do'. It requires that through faith, trust and obedience we are open to God's power ('Holy, Holy, Holy') – possible because of his promises. This power is made available to us through his Word and Spirit, and we lay hold of what he offers us, by faith in him – who is perfectly faithful – and in the finished work of Jesus upon the Cross. As disciples of Jesus we are helped by the Holy Spirit in the ongoing process of sanctification throughout our lives. Jesus prayed to his Father that we would be sanctified by his truth. His Word and his name are 'truth'. (See Isaiah **6**:3; Colossians **2**:20-22; 2 Peter **1**:3-4; Hebrews **10**:10, 14; John **17**:17; Revelation **4**:8.)

Thus, with God's correction and help, we who are 'in Christ', having been set apart for him, are to be open to the work of the Holy Spirit, and we can be sanctified increasingly. We are to love him, and being holy in all our conduct is extremely important, because our God is holy. (See Deuteronomy **6**:5; Hebrews **12**:10; 1 Peter **1**:15-16.)

18

THE VICTORIOUS LIFE – THE WILDERNESS JOURNEY

Background

The risen Lord Jesus has won the greatest victory on the cross, for us. Believers are to live in constant awareness of this, and to discover what flows from his victory in every area of their lives – as they sit with him in the heavenlies, as they walk with him in this world, and as they stand against ('resist') the enemy of our souls, who would seek to undermine the salvation our Lord has won through his finished work at Calvary. One area of the believer's walk with him where the Lord may correct and teach, and demonstrate his grace, power, and faithfulness, is in 'the wilderness'. Ephesians **2**:6; **5**:8; **6**:13; Acts **4**:12; 1 Thessalonians **5**:9–10; 2 Corinthians **12**:9.

What is 'the wilderness'? It can include those situations in life where a Christian is faced with adverse or challenging circumstances of many kinds – and it often seems to be this way *because* the believer is a follower of Jesus. There may be trials and temptations, spiritual battles to be fought. In addition, this world is, generally speaking, hostile to Jesus and the demands of the gospel. The worldly environment can sometimes be a spiritual wilderness – a desert – for the believer.

The wilderness journey is an experience many believers know, in which fresh opportunities exist to discover how to appropriate Jesus' victory in daily life, learning from and applying God's word and living in obedience to him, with the help of the Holy Spirit, as we take the path of the cross, speaking, acting and walking in the authority of Jesus' name. Mark **16**:15; Luke **9**:1–2, 23; Romans **6**:5-7, 11; **8**:1; Ephesians **6**:15; Galatians **5**:25; James **4**:7; 1 Peter **3**:15; **5**:8–9.

Wilderness situations have several features which encourage us to cry out to God. They are often dry, uninhabited places of isolation, physical or social 'deserts', with times of testing that require us to turn to God in faith and to trust him completely – and we find special places of meeting and decision. God leads his people through these places, and goes before them. He encourages them with his faithfulness, presence and grace. He will bring them into the good things that he has promised. The wilderness is a place of purpose; his tests are to refine and build up his people. Exodus **3**:8; **13**:18–22; **14**:10–11; **15**:23; Deuteronomy **8**:7; **31**:6; Joshua **1**:9; Jeremiah **31**:2; Mark **6**:31; **9**:2.

The Hebrew word *midbar* (wilderness) is derived from the root *davar*, meaning to speak or declare. God speaks to us in wilderness experiences and they are under his sovereign direction. They are normally times of testing and correction, to humble us, and to prove our love for him by whether we will listen to and obey his word or not. Jesus, too, was led into the wilderness to be tested and he gained victory over Satan with the sword of the Spirit, the word of God. Exodus **3**:1; Numbers **1**:1; Deuteronomy **8**:1-5; Matthew **4**:1-11; Mark **1**:12.

Wilderness Testing

The Lord gave his people Israel several strong tests as he led them out of Egypt and through the wilderness to the promised land of Israel. Some have overlapping significance; all have relevance for us today.

• They faced situations to which they sometimes responded in **fear**. Humanly speaking, there seemed to be the risk of failure, starvation, disease, poverty, death, though God was actually providing for all their needs. There is a kind of fear which is just worry, anxiety, but there is a proper 'fear of the

Lord', which is the beginning of wisdom. They needed the latter, not the former, and so do we. When the Israelites cried out to the Lord, he responded. *'Fear ye not, stand still and see the salvation of the LORD'* (KJV). They saw his great work, and they then feared the Lord and believed. When they called, he answered: *'Fear thou not, for I am with you'* (KJV). A proper fear of God removes our anxieties and fears about our sustenance. When we trust him, God does what seems to us to be impossible. See Exodus **3**:7–8; **14**:10–31; Isaiah **41**:10; **58**:9; Psalm **56**:3; Matthew **19**:26.

• Three days in the wilderness, and no fresh water supply had been found! They would have been worried about **thirst**. The Israelites grumbled against Moses. They should have known that the Lord would provide for them. He used a tree to make the bitter water sweet. The 'tree' of Calvary will sweeten life's hardships for the believer. If we listen diligently to our Lord's voice, and do what is right, he will protect us and heal our sicknesses – Jesus bore them for us on the cross. God's grace – his unmerited favour – sustains us. No matter why it seems as though we are going through a 'wilderness' or trials, we can still rejoice in the Lord, even in the midst of our sufferings. We are to persevere, to go on believing in Jesus and so go on having eternal life. See Exodus **15**:22–27; Isaiah **53**:4–5; **55**:1, 6; Romans **5**:1–4.

• The Israelites had been miraculously delivered from slavery in Egypt, yet now they grumbled about **food**! They missed the 'pots of meat' and plentiful food they used to have in Egypt, and now they complained against their divinely appointed leaders, Moses and Aaron. God would provide all they needed but they thought that they would go **hungry** in the wilderness. But the Lord miraculously provided sufficient food (*manna*), a kind of 'bread' from heaven. There was even extra provided so that they could observe the Sabbath without needing to work on that day. We remember that Jesus is our bread from heaven and we are fed by him. Jesus explains how this is about eternal life (see John **6**:51). Our grumbling about inconveniences and the perceived inadequacies of our circumstances may be a sign of a soul starved of time with God, and especially of 'rest' in him. It can also simply be a corrosive tendency to grumble about life, and we need to change (repent of) that whole attitude. Something in us has to change! *Do all things without murmurings . . that ye may be . . without rebuke* (KJV). See Exodus **16**:2–30; John **6**:31–32, 51; Philippians **2**:14–15. Grumbling (which may be about food supply, but can be much else!) can also show that we are not really trusting Jesus and not believing his clear explanation in John chapter 6 of why he came. So we are challenged to change any wrong ideas we have about this, and come into line with what he says; we need to understand Jesus' claims, believe him, and put into practice our professed commitment to his word. Stopping grumbling is a seemingly small but actually rather important part of what our response needs to be. It is quite obvious really: we can hardly say we are *giving thanks and rejoicing always and praying without ceasing* if at the same time we are having a grumble!

• We have begun to see that in the wilderness period, the Israelites sometimes **doubted** God's ability to keep his promises. *Is He among us or not?* (KJV) God's provision was poured out from the rock and there is living water for his people. They doubted his presence among them, yet there is persevering intercession in faith and God released victory. We enter conflict when we doubt or despair of the Lord's presence, but with faith, walking in obedience, believing and trusting in Jesus, victory over the enemy of our souls is secure. Exodus **13**:21–22; **17**:3, 7, 12; 1 Corinthians **10**:4, 12; Romans **8**:27; Hebrews **7**:25; Matthew **28**:20; Mark **9**:23; **10**:27.

• When the Israelites lost sight of God, or rejected his appointed leader, their faith wavered and they replaced God with an idol. This opened the door to worship of other gods that snared them (and sometimes it snares people today). In these days, when there are 'multi-faith' attempts to mix religions and pressures to promote the recognition of other deities, we have to consider first the *primary* application of the biblical prohibition of idolatry. We must *never* honour or give credence to any other deities. We worship only the one true God, the God of Abraham, Isaac and Jacob, who is the God and Father of our Lord Jesus Christ; we worship him as one God in three persons, Father, Son and Holy Spirit. The Ten Commandments still apply! His claim is both universal and exclusive. 'I am the way....' *Not* one of many ways!

There is a secondary implication to this (more often emphasised these days) which rightly points to the need not to exalt wealth, human fame, human ideologies or indeed anything else. Our focus should always be on God whom we praise and worship and honour. We are to beware of stubbornness, worldliness and carnality. Jesus has told us clearly, *It is written, fear/worship the Lord thy God, and serve Him only*. He gave us a desire and a command to worship, and if we put something or someone in God's place, then that other thing will become an 'idol'. In ancient times, in the wilderness, Moses pleaded for Israel. Under the new, Messianic covenant, we know that the Holy Spirit glorifies Jesus, and leads us to glorify Jesus too. Jesus is to be in the centre of our lives; and we are to go on 'abiding' in Jesus. Exodus **32**:8, 23; **31**–34; Deuteronomy **6**:13; **8**:14–17; 1 Samuel **15**:23; Matthew **4**:10; Romans **8**:7; 2 Corinthians **10**:5; James **4**:4.

We all, like sheep, have gone astray and turned to our own way (KJV). As we recognise, and are built up through what seem like 'wilderness' times, which may include tests or trials, believers in the Lord Jesus can learn to exercise faith and perseverance. Even in the face of hardship, we can learn to trust more and more in his goodness and faithfulness. We can walk closer to him who knows our infirmities, and who, like us, was . . . *in all points tempted as we are, yet without sin. Let us therefore come boldly unto the Throne of Grace that we may obtain mercy, and find Grace to help in time of need* (KJV). Isaiah **53**:6; Psalm **56**:3; Hebrews **4**:15–16.

Finally, we can be sure that, when we believers pray, we are not alone, no matter what the wilderness through which we may happen to be walking looks like to us. We can go on being filled with the Holy Spirit wherever we are and whatever is happening in our circumstances. We are privileged then to know the very presence of God with us, however we might feel. In his book entitled *Practising the Principles of Prayer*, David Pawson reminds us that in Christian prayer we are engaged with the Father, the Son and the Holy Spirit. There is a lot going on in the heavenly places, and many Christians find that true, deep intercession involves some spiritual warfare. So the desert is far from boring! Often it turns out with hindsight to have been a time for preparation for a new level or sphere of kingdom activity, as it was for Jesus after the Spirit descended on him, but before his public ministry really began. So if your wilderness seems a bit bleak or full of temptations, don't be discouraged by that, remember that God leads his people out of it, and that you may look back on it as having been a time of training for something else; and in any event God wants your walk with him to become stronger.

19

THE VICTORIOUS LIFE — ABSOLUTE SURRENDER

Background

The victorious life is the gift of the Lord Jesus to every believer. It may be summed up in this affirmation in Paul's letter to believers in Rome: *Therefore, there is now no condemnation for those who are in Christ Jesus, because through Christ Jesus the law of the Spirit who gives life has set you free from the law of sin and death.* This freedom from death (death being the wages of sin), and God's gift of eternal life through the Lord Jesus, was achieved when God sent his own Son, who knew no sin, and *made Him to be sin for us . . that we might be made the righteousness of God in Him* (KJV). Jesus' death upon the cross secures victory over sin in our lives, if we are 'in Christ Jesus', and 'walk after the Spirit'. Our response to this amazing gift of love is to offer to the Lord, in thanks, a life of absolute surrender, with *our mind governed by the Spirit, which is life and peace.* Romans **6**:23; **8**:1–6; **12**:1; 2 Corinthians **5**:21; Colossians **3**:15.

Absolute surrender, however, is not inactivity or apathy. When we totally surrender to God, and submit every area of our life to him, he quickens us, in spirit, soul and body, for his service. He puts a new heart and a new spirit within us; having said: *and I will put My Spirit within you* (KJV). This is the victorious life, when his Spirit has total freedom in us to do his will. The Lord calls us to submit three crucial areas to him: his Lordship, our obedience and our love. Ezekiel **36**:26–27; 1 Corinthians **6**:17–20; 1 Thessalonians **5**:23.

Lordship

There are over 250 titles of the Lord Jesus in Scripture. In the Gospels, the most frequent appellation is 'Lord'. He is the Lord over all creation, of the living and the dead, and of his church. The decision to acknowledge him for who he is (Maker and upholder of the universe, and the source of life), and for what he has done (laid down his life for us), and to receive his gift of eternal life, is a vital step for new believers. We are encouraged in this to humble ourselves before him and to cast every care and burden upon him, for he desires our peace with him. John **13**:13; Acts **2**:36; Revelation **19**:16; Colossians **1**:16; Romans **14**:9; Ephesians **5**:23; Hebrews **1**:2–3; **11**:3; Genesis **1**:30; **2**:7; Psalm **139**:14–16. John **6**:68; 1 Peter **5**:6–7; Jeremiah **29**:11.

If (as Thomas affirmed) Jesus is, *'my Lord and my God'*, then I will give him every area of my life to rule over, as King and Lord, and allow his Spirit to keep me on the path of holiness and obedience, often through the Father's correction in love. Leviticus **20**:7; Deuteronomy **4**:30–31; Psalm **89**:14–18; John **14**:15, 23; **20**:28; Acts **5**:32; 2 Corinthians **6**:17; Ephesians **1**:4; Hebrews **5**:9; **12**:9–11.

Obedience

The Bible underlines the importance of hearing the voice of the Lord and obeying his instructions and commandments. The important text known as the *Sh'ma* (Deuteronomy **6**:4–9) is so called after the first word of Deuteronomy **6**:4, which means 'Hear' in the sense of 'Obey'. This injunction is relevant today to individuals, churches and nations. God has set before us *life and death, blessings and cursings*, and says, *Now choose life, so that you and your children may live . . may love the Lord your God . . may obey His voice . . and may hold fast to Him: for He is your life*. We know that if we keep God's laws, that is proof that we love him. Those who trust him in faith will obey him. When we listen and obey him all the blessings listed in Deuteronomy 28 will not just come upon us, but overtake us. But if we will not listen to his voice and observe the law of Christ we show that we do not love him, and not only hinder his blessings but bring ourselves under a curse.

Because Abraham obeyed God's voice, all nations of the earth have been blessed through his descendants. When the people of Israel obeyed God's voice, he protected them from sickness, and from their enemies. Our obedience to Jesus as the Lord of our life is part of our surrender to him and of our victorious walk in the Spirit. Genesis **22**:18; Exodus **15**:26; **23**:22; Deuteronomy **11**:26–29; **28**:1–68; **30**:19–20; Isaiah **50**:10; Luke **11**:28; John **14**:21; Hebrews **11**:8.

Love

The principal way of showing our love for and obedience to the Lord Jesus is to know his commandments and keep them; this is accompanied by the most wonderful promises – that the Father will love us, Jesus will manifest himself to us and make his dwelling with us. This brings us his peace and joy, and dispels anxiety and fear. Jesus loved and obeyed the Father; we are to love and obey the Son. As he abides in the Father's love, so are we to abide in his love, fulfilling God's command to love him with all our heart [including our will and mind; pursuing good and rejecting evil], all our soul [including our emotions and desires – even the desire to hold on to our life] and all our strength [including resources, time, wealth, belongings, skills, energy, etc.], and to love our neighbour as ourselves. Deuteronomy **6**:5; Mark **12**:28–34; John **12**:23–26; **14**:15–**15**:27; Revelation **12**:11.

So mature believers who want to be Jesus' disciples in absolute surrender, walking in obedience to and love of the Lord of lords and King of kings, must fulfil his requirements, so that they may live lives worthy of him – denying themselves (saying 'No' to their own will), taking up their cross daily (which sometimes entails suffering), following him (having counted the cost first); hearing his voice *and* doing his will. Jesus submitted totally to his Father's will. Our victory in him is to be found through an absolute surrender to his will, in holiness and obedience to him (that we may abide in him), so that we might be clean *vessels unto honour, sanctified, and meet for the Master's use, and prepared unto every good work* (KJV). *For we preach Jesus Christ as Lord . . [to show] the light of the knowledge of God's glory displayed in the face of Christ . . and we have this treasure in jars of clay to show that this all-surpassing power is from God, and not from us.*

Matthew **7**:24; **10**:38; **26**:39; Luke **8**:21; **9**:23; John **4**:34; **5**:19 (KJV); **10**:27; **13**:37; Romans **6**:6–7; 2 Corinthians **4**:5–7; 2 Timothy **2**:20–21; Hebrews **10**:5–10.

20
TEMPTATION

Background

The word 'temptation' refers to the tendency and enticement either by Satan or by man's unregenerate nature ('the flesh') to provide opportunity for sin, which is rebellion against God. Temptation focuses on the desires and cravings of human nature, rather than doing what is right in God's sight. No human being is above being tempted or taking opportunity for sin. The Bible distinguishes between, on the one hand, *temptation* (that is common to man, and not, in itself, sin) which is always Satan-initiated, is aimed at drawing us into sin, and brings guilt and failure, and separates us from God – to pull us down – and, on the other hand, *testing*, which is allowed by God, but with the object of teaching us endurance and strengthening our faith – to build us up.

Genesis **4**:7; **26**:10; 1 Kings **22**:21; Nehemiah **9**:17; Psalm **106**:14; Isaiah **59**:2; Luke **22**:31; John **16**:8; 1 Corinthians **10**:13; James **1**:12-14.

Temptation

God does not tempt anyone. It is Satan's desire through temptation to entice man into sin by his own lust (the desire to do what is prohibited in God's Word) and thus break fellowship with the holy God. Sin, in fulness, then brings death.

Deuteronomy **5**:7–21; Isaiah **59**:2; Romans **6**:23; James **1**:13–15.

Scripture records, for our instruction, biblical figures who fell into sin through temptation. Examples include Adam and Eve (pride, through acceptance of Satan's lie), Abraham (through fear), David (through pride, and later lust and murder), Peter (through self-pride), and Ananias (through willingness to seek to deceive the apostle concerning money). The major sources of temptation are: demonic enticement; the deception of man's desire for self-gratification, self-justification, human pride and power; and the rebellious nature of the world's value system.

Genesis **3**:4–5; **11**:4; **12**:13; **14**:4; Leviticus **26**:19; Numbers **20**:2; **27**:14; Deuteronomy **8**:18; 1 Samuel **13**:11–13a; 2 Samuel **11**:2–4; **11**:15; 2 Samuel **13**:11–14; 1 Chronicles **21**:1–3; Matthew **20**:21; **23**:27; Acts **5**:2–3, 9; 1 Timothy **3**:3; James **4**:4; 1 John **2**:16; Revelation **12**:9.

Examples of biblical figures who rejected temptation include: Abraham (who took no reward from the king of Sodom); Elisha (who refused payment for healing); Peter (who rejected money from Simon to buy a spiritual gift); and, of course, supremely, the Lord Jesus (who defeated Satan's attempt to entrap him with the Word of God). The main strategy by which Satan tries to draw us into temptation is to get us to believe a lie, and accept licence by doubting the truth of God's Word.

Genesis **14**:21-24; 2 Kings **5**:16; Matthew **4**:3-10; John **8**:44; Acts **8**:20-21.

To combat temptation it is necessary to recognise our weaknesses; avoid opportunity for sin; quench the fiery darts of the enemy by our faith in God and his promises; reject the world-value system by submitting to the Lord Jesus, and resisting Satan with the Word of God. God promises a way to escape from temptation, and we can repent quickly when we fall.

To stand against the wiles of the devil we must humble ourselves and not be ignorant of his devices, put on the whole armour of God, believe and trust his Word, and pray at all times.

Genesis **39**:12; Matthew **26**:41; John **4**:50 (KJV); 1

Corinthians **10**:13; 2 Corinthians **2**:11; Ephesians **6**:11–18; James **4**:7; 1 Peter **5**:6-9; 1 John **5**:4; Revelation **2**:5.

Testings

The testing times that God gives are primarily to know what is in man's heart (rather than to entice into sin) and to prove or test whether a person will obey his commandments and instructions or not. Man's rebellion in tempting God or putting him to the test is sin. This always results in judgment, and, for some, entry to their promised land is denied.

Exodus **16**:4; **17**:7–8; Numbers **14**:22–23; Deuteronomy **6**:16; **8**:2; **11**:16; Psalm **78**:18, 21-22; **106**:14; Matthew **4**:7.

Abraham was tested when God told him to offer his promised son Isaac as a sacrifice at Mount Moriah, yet he believed God's goodness. Job was tested by the removal of all he had, yet by faith acknowledged God's purpose in his suffering. Both were given a vision of resurrection. Moses was tested through the rebellion of the people of Israel, and Hezekiah was tested on account of his foolishness. Nations are also tested, as when Israel's enemies were left nearby, to see whether Israel would obey the Lord and keep to his way. God's purpose in these testings of the righteous and of the rebellious was to refine their character, so they might listen to him and walk more closely in his ways, so that he might bless them.

Genesis **22**:1–2, 5-8; Exodus **17**:2–8; Numbers **20**:8–12; Judges **2**:21–23; **3**:1, 4; 2 Chronicles **32**:31; Job **19**:25–26; **23**:8–10; Psalm **66**:10–12; **95**:8; Isaiah **48**:10; Jeremiah **9**:7; Daniel **11**:35; Malachi **3**:2–3.

Paul was given a 'thorn in the flesh' to keep him from pride (from being '*exalted above measure*') to remind him, even as he was serving the Lord with great humility and in severe testing, that, *My grace is sufficient for you, for My power is made perfect in weakness . . .* that the power of Christ might rest upon him. See Acts **20**:19; 2 Corinthians **12**:7–9 (KJV); Galatians **4**:14.

Those who endure testings will receive a crown of life, because endurance demonstrates a love for Jesus, and trains his disciples to be overcomers. God helps us to endure temptations and testings by providing a way out. He knows how to rescue the godly from trials. Jesus has overcome the world, and since the One that is in us is greater than the one who is in the world, our faith in the Son of God secures our victory as overcomers. These disciples overcame Satan *by the Blood of the Lamb, by the word of their testimony, and they did not . . shrink from death*. Jesus has many promises for those who overcome. If we patiently endure, we will receive a crown that will last for ever.

1 Corinthians **9**:25; **10**:13; James **1**:12; 2 Peter **2**:9; Revelation chapters **2** and **3**; **12**:11.

21

GOD

Background

The Bible begins with the assertion that God created the heavens and the earth, which means that he created *everything*. We learn that he is pre-existent and uncreated. It is *the fool* and *the wicked* who deny his existence (Psalm **10**:4, **14**:1, **15**:1).

We can deduce some truths about him from what he has made. For example, Paul states very clearly that since the creation of the world God's eternal power and divine nature have been clearly seen. That he is who he is can be understood by all, because all of us can see what he has made (see Romans **1**:18). That is precisely why mankind's thanklessness and moral depravity means that we are 'without excuse'. Beyond that fundamental truth which all mankind should see, there is God's self-revelation through the Scriptures he caused to be written (see Unit 42), and supremely in his incarnation in his Son, Jesus Christ.

Names by which God is revealed in Scripture

One way of discovering truths about God is through considering the names by which he is designated in the Bible. (See Note 1.)

ELOHIM = The all powerful one (plural). This is used 2,500 times in the Old Testament. (See Note 2 below.)

EL = The singular form of Elohim and indicates 'the strong one'. Cf. Genesis **16**:13; **46**:3, etc.

EL-ELYON = 'God Most High', the ultimate and supreme

Being who is the Creator and rightful owner of all that exists (Genesis **14**:18–22; cf. Luke **2**:14).

EL-SHADDAI = 'God Almighty who is God All-Mercy.' 'Shaddai' derives from a word for 'mountain' and for 'breast', as well as from a verb meaning 'to be irresistibly strong' – thus combining the idea of immovable might with the notion of unshakeable tenderness (e.g. Genesis **17**:1; **28**:3–4; **49**:25).

EL-OLAM = 'the Everlasting God' (Genesis **21**:33).

YAHWEH (or 'Jehovah', 'Yah') = 'the ever-existent One', 'the One who was and is and is to come', the 'I AM' – usually represented as 'LORD' (in capitals) in English Bibles. This is God's covenant name and is used about 7,000 times in the Scriptures (e.g. Genesis **2**:4; Exodus **3**:14–15; Malachi **3**:6; cf. also John **8**:58; Hebrews **13**:8).

JEHOVAH-ELOHIM (or 'LORD God') = 'the I AM who is Almighty' (e.g. Genesis **2**:4).

JEHOVAH-JIREH = 'the LORD will see/provide' – the God who sees, cares and provides what is needed for deliverance (Genesis **22**:13–14).

JEHOVAH-ROPHI = 'the LORD who is healer' (Exodus **15**:26; cf. also Matthew **4**:23, **9**:35).

JEHOVAH-NISSI = 'the LORD is my banner', or 'the LORD is my Lifted-Up One' (Exodus **17**:8–15; cf. also John **3**:14–15).

JEHOVAH-SHALOM = 'the LORD is Peace' (Judges **6**:24; cf. also Isaiah **9**:6; Ephesians **2**:14).

JEHOVAH-ROI = 'the LORD my Shepherd' (e.g. Psalm **23**; cf. also John **10**:11–15).

JEHOVAH-TSIDKENU = 'the LORD our Righteousness' (Jeremiah **23**:6, **33**:16; cf. also 1 Corinthians **1**:30).

JEHOVAH-SHAMMAH = 'the LORD is there' (Ezekiel **48**:35).

JEHOVAH-SEBAOTH = 'the Lord of hosts/armies' – the LORD who commands the angelic hosts and all the powers of heaven and earth. God is not called this until 1 Samuel **1**:3, in the time of Israel's need, but it is his title frequently from then on, e.g. 80 times in Jeremiah and 14 times in two chapters of Haggai (1 Samuel **1**:3; Psalm **24**:10; **46**:7, 11; Isaiah **6**:1-5; **44**:6; Malachi **3**:16–17; Luke **2**:13; Matthew **26**:53; James **5**:4).

The Bible reveals other attributes of God

Omnipresence = 'He cannot be avoided' (Psalm **139**:7–10; Jeremiah **23**:24; Acts **17**:24–28).

Omnipotence = 'He cannot be overcome' (Job **42**:2; Jeremiah **32**:17; Psalm **33**:6–9; Matthew **19**:26; Nahum **1**:3).

Omniscience = 'He cannot be deceived' (Psalm **139**:1–6; 1 John **3**:20; Psalm **147**:4–5; cf. also John **2**:24–25).

Transcendence = 'He cannot be excelled' (Genesis **21**:33; 2 Chronicles **6**:18; 1 Timothy **1**:17).

God is *good* – revealed in creation (Genesis **1**:31) and in his being 'gracious' or 'kind' (Exodus **34**:6–7; 2 Chronicles **30**:9; Psalm **103**:8–14; Mark **10**:18).

God is *love* – (See 1 John **4**:8–16.) The Greek word used for 'love' in this passage is 'agape' which has a very special meaning. It does not signify 'eros' love. Believers are reminded in this passage that something good and undeserved has been done for them in the death and resurrection of Jesus, saving them from the penalty of past sin; it does not mean that we are attractive to God or inherently lovable.

God is *holy* – (See Leviticus **19**:2; Isaiah **6**:3; cf. also John **8**:46; Hebrews **4**:15.) Holiness has at least two very important biblical dimensions: it speaks to us again of the 'otherness' or transcendence of God (and as we recall this we see the sinfulness of worshipping created things rather than the Creator himself), and it reminds us also that God is absolutely perfect. It is easy to see how this fits with the biblically revealed truth that he is perfectly *just* in all his ways and judgements. So he cannot tolerate sin. In justice, sin must be punished. That is not cruel. It is not unfair. This is the key reason why we need to know, believe in and trust Jesus Christ and his sacrifice. Only his blood shed for us will open up the way to the one holy and just God. We all need to receive his forgiveness for all our sins. So we need to come to Christ and trust in him alone to save us from the penalty for our sin. Otherwise our sins would lead to death and hell, and that would be entirely our own fault. If that seems to us to be harsh, it is because our own sinful nature makes it hard for us to see what perfect holiness would look like. Can we imagine a world in which there is no injustice, no cruelty, no sin whatsoever? That is the sort of world God is determined to have! It is his (agape) love that has provided the way of salvation.

God is *Spirit* – (See John **4**:24.) This great revelation is linked by Jesus to true *worship*. The Jews already knew that idolatry, the worship of created objects, was utterly wrong. We learn here that we need to be open to the work of the Holy Spirit, not least as we worship, and that we must worship God '...*in truth*'. This reminds us that to worship we must be *in* Christ (who is *himself* the truth, as he told us). Hypocritical and merely outward 'worship' which is not genuine obviously has no value. The true worshipper must be walking in obedience to Christ having repented (turned away from) sin and must be *going on believing* in Jesus (which, as we have learnt, is about a personal relationship, not merely believing propositions *about* him).

In the centuries since the closure of the canon of Scripture, Christians have continued to think and talk about the nature of God. These reflections have sometimes become philosophical and often very abstract. So there is today a great deal that passes for 'theology' which lacks authenticity precisely because it all too often departs from God's self-revelation. (See Note 2.)

Note 1

ELOHIM – Hebrew nouns have a dual form for 2 and a plural form for 3 or more. In Genesis 1:1 *Elohim* is in this plural form (indicating that God is a Trinity of Being [cf. *"us"* in Genesis **1**:26–27 & Isaiah **6**:8]) and governs a verb in the singular (indicating that he is one God [cf. Deuteronomy 6:4, where *"one"* in the Hebrew indicates unity]). During the course of the Bible the unity of the Godhead in three persons (Father, Son and Holy Spirit) is progressively revealed, and it eventually becomes clear that (prior to his Incarnation) God the Son was seen as the divine Angel of the Lord who appears from time to time (e.g. Genesis **16**:7,10,13; Exodus **23**:20–21). 'Elohim' means 'the all-powerful one' and is used around 2,500 times in the Old Testament.

Note 2

See also: *The Nature of God*, chapter 2 from the book *The Empty Promise of Godism*, also available as a downloadable PDF on the Glory to Glory website.

22

CHRIST

Background

God the Son (the second person of the Trinity) became a human being. He was and is truly divine and truly human; he is the only Saviour of fallen men and women. So he was named 'Jesus' ('Yah [Jehovah] is Salvation'). He came to live a perfect life and die on the cross as the substitute for sinners so that they might be reconciled with God (cf. 2 Corinthians **5**:17–21). To do this he had to be the 'anointed one' ('Messiah' from the Hebrew or 'Christ' from the Greek). Though born in Bethlehem, as God he was in existence before his human birth and indeed even before the creation of the world (cf. John **1**:1–3; **8**:56-58; **17**:5, 24; Philippians **2**:6; Colossians **1**:15–16; **2**:9; Hebrews **1**:2–3). Jesus Christ is LORD!

The Old Testament

The Old Testament foretells Christ's first coming. (See Psalm **110**:1; Isaiah **9**:6–7; **42**:1–3 [cf. Matthew **12**:18–21]; Daniel **9**:25; Malachi **3**:1–2.) At various points in the Old Testament, occasions are recorded which are interpreted by some as signifying that the Son of God appeared to people before his Incarnation – 'Christophanies'.

Prophets, priests and kings were anointed, and Jesus was anointed to hold all those three offices – he was anointed with the Holy Spirit (not oil); and his crown was made of thorns (not gold and jewels).

Leviticus **8**:12 (cf. Hebrews **4**:14); Deuteronomy **18**:15,18–19 (cf. Acts **3**:22–26); 1 Samuel **16**:12–13; 2 Samuel **7**:16 (cf.

Luke **1**:32–33); Psalm **110**:4 (cf. Hebrews **5**:6,10); Isaiah **61**:1–2 (cf. Luke **4**:18–19); Zechariah **9**:9; Matthew **1**:1, 23; **2**:1–6; **3**:16–17; **21**:5; **27**:29.

His Holy Life

Adam, the first man, disobeyed God and drew all humanity into his sinfulness – see Genesis chapter 3. Jesus, the Son of God (born of the Virgin Mary in Bethlehem) became the second Adam but did not succumb to sin. Jesus Christ fulfilled all righteousness and went about doing nothing but good.

Isaiah **7**:13–14; Micah **5**:2; Matthew **1**:23; Luke **1**:35; John **8**:46; Acts **10**:38; 1 Corinthians **15**:45; 2 Corinthians **5**:21; Hebrews **4**:15; 1 Peter **2**:22.

His Atoning Death – the Crucifixion

For six terrible hours Jesus hung upon the cross, voluntarily dying for the sins of mankind. Although he was in indescribable physical pain, in an even more terrible way he was in a position of temporary alienation from his Father – because he was the sin-bearer for us. This is something that no human can truly understand (see Matthew **27**:45). Jesus looked out over the city that had cast him out to die. The soldiers at his feet threw dice for his clothes. The priests were glad at their 'victory'. The holiday crowd looked on. 'The world in type and reality was there before him – the world for which he was dying.' (Joe Church)

Because of the perfect humanity and divinity of Jesus, he was able to offer himself on the cross as the substitute for sinners, bearing the penalty for their sins, making it possible for fallen people to be reconciled to God – redeemed people, members of his body.

Psalm **22**:1–21; Isaiah **50**:4–7; **52**:13–**53**:12; Zechariah **11**:10–13; **13**:7; Matthew **20**:28; **21**:42; **26**:31; **27**:9–10, 29; 33–50; Mark **15**:22–39; Luke **23**:27–48; John **12**:32;

19:17–19; Romans **4**:25; **5**:6–11; 2 Corinthians **5**:17–21; Galatians **3**:13.

His Life-Giving Exaltation

The astonishing work of Christ went further than dealing with the objective guilt of sinners, and death, the penalty for sin. By the resurrection and exaltation of Jesus Christ, and through the work of the promised Holy Spirit, the pardoned are given new spiritual life. By adoption and grace, believers can now know the Spirit of sonship (see Romans **8**:15). The only-begotten Son of God, the Son of Man, was raised from the dead and exalted – now those who are led by the Spirit can cry, 'Abba, Father'.

Acts **1**:8; Romans **8**:15; Galatians **4**:5; Ephesians **1**:5; **11**:26; 1 John **2**:27.

His Second Coming to Reign

Moreover, the exalted Christ will one day return as King and Judge of all, thus ushering in a new order. Jesus Christ is 'King of kings and Lord of lords'. Every knee shall bow before him.

Matthew **24**:27–31, 39; **25**:31–46; Acts **1**:9–11; **17**:31; 1 Timothy **6**:14–16; 2 Timothy **4**:8; Revelation **11**:15; **17**:14; **19**:16.

Jesus is also given other titles in Scripture which further reveal his character

EMMANUEL = *God with us* (Isaiah **7**:14; Matthew **1**:23).

THE WORD = *Logos*. To the Hebrews, a word was more than a mere sound, it had active power – as when God spoke the world into existence (Genesis 1). To the Greeks, 'logos' meant both the 'inward' thought and its 'outward' expression. Since the Son of God is God and his manifestation in human form, we can see that 'the Word' was a perfect title for Christ – God making himself actively known to mankind. John

1:1–4; Hebrews **1**:3; Revelation **19**:13.

THE LORD 'Kurios' [Yahweh/Jehovah]. See Luke **10**:1; John **21**:7; Acts **10**:36; Romans **1**:4; **10**:9; 1 Corinthians **15**:57; Philippians **2**:11.

SON OF GOD A title highlighting his deity. See Matthew **4**:3, 6; **27**:43; Mark **15**:39; Luke **1**:35; **22**:70; John **1**:14, **3**:16; Philippians **2**:5–11; Titus **2**:13; Revelation **2**:18.

SON OF MAN A title highlighting his humanity (some 80 times in the New Testament). See Daniel **7**:13–14; Matthew **8**:20; **24**:37–44; Luke **19**:10; John **3**:13.

LAMB OF GOD The substitutionary sacrifice for sinners, the ultimate Passover Lamb. See John **1**:29, 36; 1 Corinthians **5**:7.

LAST ADAM The source of a new redeemed humanity – to those who will trust in him as Saviour. See 1 Corinthians **15**:45–49.

Note

For more free material on Jesus, see the Glory to Glory Publications' website, and *The Birth of Christ*, particularly chapter 6.

23

THE HOLY SPIRIT

Background

The Holy Spirit (the third person of the Trinity) is as truly God as God the Father and God the Son. Though the Hebrew and Greek words for 'Spirit' also mean 'wind' and 'breath', he is *personal*, not just an influence or energy or mode of action, and he can be grieved (Ephesians **4**:30). As God the Holy One, he will never prompt us to say or do anything that is ungodly and contrary to the Bible, which he himself caused to be written (cf. 2 Peter **1**:20–21; 1 Thessalonians **2**:13). Not only must he be reverenced as God, Jesus himself said that it is unpardonable for us to blaspheme him (Matthew **12**:31). Rejection of the Spirit would be rejection of the very person who applies God's grace to our lives.

Psalm **139**:7–10; Matthew **28**:19; Luke **1**:35; John **14**:26; **15**:26; Acts **1**:8; **5**:3; Romans **8**:26–27; Galatians **4**:6; Ephesians **4**:30; Hebrews **9**:14; 1 John **4**:1–3.

Old Testament

The Holy Spirit was active in creation. The Spirit was present to believers (cf. Psalm **51**:11) and would act upon God's human agents (temporarily) to equip them for divine tasks. There was also the promise that the Spirit would one day be in believers to enliven and empower them 'from the inside'.

Genesis **1**:2 [cf. Job **33**:4; Psalm **104**:30], Genesis **6**:3; Exodus **31**:3; Numbers **11**:26–29; **24**:2; Judges **3**:10; **6**:34; **13**:24–25; **14**:19; **15**:14; 1 Samuel **10**:6; **11**:6; **16**:14; 2 Samuel **23**:2; 1 Chronicles **12**:18; **28**:12; 2 Chronicles **24**:20; Nehemiah **9**:30; Isaiah **32**:15; **42**:1; **44**:3; **61**:1; **63**:10; Ezekiel **36**:26–27; Joel **2**:28–29; Zechariah **4**:6.

The Gospels

In the Gospels the work of the Holy Spirit was manifested powerfully in and through Christ. So Jesus could tell the disciples that the Holy Spirit dwelt *with* them and would one day be *in* them (John **14**:15–18). The indwelling of the Spirit would be a glorious result of Christ's atoning work and resurrection. Then it would be possible for believers to be born again and share in the life of the risen and glorified Christ. On the day of his resurrection, Jesus made this a reality for his disciples: 'He breathed on them and said, "*Receive the Holy Spirit.*"' (John **20**:22; the Greek verb means, 'Receive now'). They were changed! (cf. their story up to the end of Acts 1). Jesus also taught his disciples that, when he departed from them, the Holy Spirit would come to be with them as another helper/advocate/counsellor/comforter (Greek *parakletos*). The Holy Spirit would come upon disciples, empowering them to be his witnesses throughout the world. Believers would be baptised in the Holy Spirit (see Matthew **3**:11; Acts **1**:5; **11**:15–17). This was not without a visible effect! A gift of tongues was normative in the early church and has been known and experienced by countless believers since then. Equipping for service and mission is vital for members of Christ's body, the church (see 1 Corinthians **12**:13).

Matthew **1**:18; **10**:20; Luke **1**:15; **2**:25–27; **3**:16, 22; **4**:1; **11**:13; John **3**:5–8; **7**:37–39; **15**:26; **16**:7–15.

N.B. Though the word for 'Spirit' (*pneuma*) is a neuter noun in Greek and a feminine noun in Hebrew, Jesus strikingly disregards all that and refers to the Spirit as 'he' (*ekeinos* – emphatic masculine pronoun): John **15**:26; **16**:13–15.

From the Day of Pentecost onwards

The Holy Spirit is now 'with', 'in' and 'upon' the true believers. See John **3**:3-8; Acts **2**:1–38; **4**:8, 31; **7**:55; **8**:14–17; **10**:44–48; **13**:2–4; **19**:2–7; Romans **8**:9–11; 1 John **2**:20, 27.

The work of the Holy Spirit

The work of the Holy Spirit in the life of the believer and of the church is expounded in the epistles. 'Religion' without the Holy Spirit would be dead. It is the Spirit who gives life (see 2 Corinthians **3**:6). The Spirit produces in the believer the character of Christ – the 'fruit' (singular!) described in Galatians **5**:22–23.

Romans **5**:5; **8**:1–27; **14**:17; 1 Corinthians **2**:4, 10–14; **3**:16; 2 Corinthians **3**:3–6, 17; Galatians **3**:1 –5, 14; **4**:29; **5**:16–26; Ephesians **4**:3–4, 30; **6**:17–18; Philippians **1**:18–19; **2**:1; **3**:3; 1 Thessalonians **5**:19; 2 Thessalonians **2**:13; 1 Timothy **4**:1; 2 Timothy **1**:13–14; Titus **3**:4–6; Hebrews **9**:14; 1 Peter **4**:14; 2 Peter **1**:21; 1 John **3**:24; Jude **20**; Revelation **3**:22.

[Some believers are persuaded that the 'gifts of the Spirit' (Greek *charismata*, as in 1 Corinthians **12**:4–11) were only given to the early church, to establish the first Christians until the New Testament was complete. In fact the New Testament nowhere says that the charismatic gifts are temporary. They are needed just as much today.]

Discernment is needed

Christians need to be aware that not everything that happens which is *claimed* as a manifestation of the Spirit is always actually his doing. We need to exercise discernment and humility at all times, weighing what we see in the light of Scripture, and not jump to conclusions when we are unsure or uneasy. Christians need to remember that our enemy uses the counterfeit to lead people astray. That cautionary note having been sounded, we are to be open to the work of the Holy Spirit. We are to be baptised in Holy Spirit; we are to go on being filled with him; we are not to grieve him; we are to be sensitive to his prompting. He is our counsellor. We have been given in the New Testament examples of how he operates. We know that he convicts of sin, righteousness and judgement (see John **16**:7–11) and he always glorifies Jesus. The fruit of the Holy Spirit (listed by Paul in Galatians

5:22–26) and the gifts of the Spirit (listed by Paul in 1 Corinthians **12**:4–11) are both still needed by believers today.

Unusual manifestations may sometimes be visible in some who are experiencing the impact of the Holy Spirit in Christian gatherings, and what we see happening may be how a person is *reacting to* the presence and activity of the Spirit.

It is very important that no believer should think it is somehow spiritually superior to be manifesting a particular outward physical reaction! Pastors will be aware of this, and are in special need of wisdom and discernment as they lead and minister, and train others to do so.

A concluding thought

Many Christians, either because of ignorance or through degrees of carelessness in their discipleship, do not enter into all the blessings available to them in their walk on the Way. Believers need teaching, training and pastoring. Furthermore, we all tend to 'leak' – some lose what was once enjoyed, growing weary, falling into sinful behaviour and grieving the Holy Spirit. So we need to heed again Paul's exhortation: *Go on being filled with Spirit* (Ephesians **5**:18).

24

LAW

Background

The word 'law' makes us think of legislation and law courts, but the Hebrew word *torah* actually means 'teaching' or 'instruction'. The moment Adam and Eve fell into sin they were estranged from the righteous God and needed instruction about how they could now approach the Lord without being consumed in the fire of his holy wrath. No matter how hard people tried to live God-pleasing lives, as fallen creatures they fell into sin. As sinners, they needed a way of forgiveness and of reconciliation with God, and that was always on the basis of blood sacrifice – pointing forward to Calvary. It is clear from Genesis **4**:3–7 that Abel was bringing his sacrifice in response to divine instruction (it involved the shedding of the blood of the firstborn of the flock and the burning of fat portions), whereas Cain ignored those instructions and brought an inevitably unacceptable offering of the fruit of the ground (which represented his own supposedly 'meritorious' works). This is how things remained until the Exodus.

At Sinai

Following on from the marvellous deliverance of the people of Israel through the Passover and the crossing of the Red Sea, the saved Israelites needed instruction in how to live righteous lives as God's covenant people. The Law (known as 'the Law of Moses') was not given as the means of salvation but as the response to it – just as Abraham had first been saved by faith (he 'believed the Lord'; Genesis **15**:5–6) and was called to live a holy life in a covenant relationship with God (Genesis **17**:1–14).

The Ten Commandments begin with a reminder of salvation and covenant grace before they give a succinct summary of what it means to live in a God-pleasing and God-honouring way (see Exodus **20**:1–17). In Exodus to Deuteronomy the Law was spelled out in great detail, as was the sacrificial system which would deal with the guilt incurred by not keeping the Law. Indeed, the Law could not make God's people perfect: it functioned not only as the goal of righteousness but also as the straight edge to reveal that: 'all have sinned and fall' [lit. 'go on falling'] 'short of the glory of God' (Romans **3**:23). Paul calls it the *paidagogos* – the 'instructor/guide/guardian/trainer' of boys whose task it was to educate them to virtuous maturity. The Law was intended to lead people to Christ as Saviour (Galatians **3**:24–27). Sadly, the Jews did not see true righteousness as the fruit of faith but sought to earn merit under the Law, only to fail (see Romans **9**:31–32).

Exodus **20**:1–26; **24**:12; **31**:18; Deuteronomy **6**:6–9; Psalm **1**:1–2; **19**:7–11; **37**:27–31; **40**:8–10; **119**:1–8; John **7**:19; Romans **10**:1ff; Galatians **3**:11–29.

Law can never make people righteous before God. It can show us what is good, but it cannot enable us to do it. It is about external duty, not an inner power. It brings condemnation, not peace with God. Our only hope of righteousness is to be changed on the inside (regeneration and conversion, and then continuing in faith, obedience and perseverance). Grace makes all this possible.

Isaiah **1**:13–18; **5**:24; Jeremiah **9**:13–16; Ezekiel **22**:26; Daniel **9**:8–13; Matthew **22**:36–40; Luke **1**:6; Acts **13**:39; **15**:5,10–11; Romans **2**:12–14; **3**:20; **4**:15; **5**:13–14; **8**:3–4; Galatians **3**:21; Philippians **3**:4, 6; Hebrews **7**:19; James **2**:10.

Good news! Jesus Christ, God the Son incarnate, Son of Man, lived a sinless life and fulfilled all righteousness as our representative (the second and last Adam, the head of redeemed humanity). Having atoned for our sins through his substitutionary sacrifice on the Cross, the risen and glorified Christ imputes and imparts his own righteousness to those who repent, are baptised and go on believing and trusting in him for salvation. Moreover, he comes to dwell in us through the Holy Spirit and so enables us to live holy lives. Interestingly, the Greek word for 'law' (like the English word) means both 'statute' and 'principle' (like the 'law' of gravity) – outer duty and inner dynamic. The 'law of Christ' is seen in righteous living in a believer (see Galatians **6**:2) which reflects something of the goodness which we see perfectly in Jesus himself. In the New Testament, believers are called 'saints' (God's holy ones who are set apart to live to his glory). We are saved by grace through faith, and we live by grace as the Holy Spirit aids us in our walk of obedience to Jesus.

Matthew **5**:17; John **1**:17; Acts **9**:13 (and often afterwards); Acts **15**:11; Romans **7**:7–**8**:11; **13**:8–10; Ephesians **2**:4–10; Philippians **2**:12–13.

The grace of God revealed in the gospel is not to be an excuse for careless living. Indeed, if we turn back from the gospel, we are apostates and come under God's righteous judgement.

Acts **15**:1–2, 5, 19–20; Romans **6**:1–14; Galatians **3**:10; **5**:3–6; Hebrews **6**:4–6.

25

LOVE

Background: the different kinds of 'love'

'Love' is a term that is often encountered in Christian theology and ethics. However, we must note at the outset that as a word in the English language it is very ambiguous, covering disparate meanings. It is used to translate a number of different words from the Greek New Testament, each of which has a different meaning in the original language there. So there is scope for a great deal of confusion and misunderstanding.

In biblical usage there is a strongly moral sense to this word – something often forgotten by those who sentimentalise biblical references to the love of God (of which there are fewer than many Christians imagine). Of the Greek words that are now loosely translated as 'love', *eros* (sexual attraction/love) does not appear in the New Testament. The Greek *phileo*, signifying natural affection (with more feeling than reason) occurs twenty-five times, with *philadelphia* (brotherly love) five times, and *philia* (friendship) occurring in James **4**:4, but also, very importantly (from the same *phileo* root) in the last two of Jesus' three questions addressed to Peter in John 21. By far the most frequent Greek biblical word translated into English as 'love' is *agape*, generally taken to signify a moral good rather than attraction. Agape includes doing good to the undeserving and the unattractive person. It can involve meeting a need. The difference between *agape* and *phileo* may be difficult to comprehend in all passages. (See Note 1.)

True love does not come naturally to fallen man (e.g. the love that causes a man to pray for his enemies; Matthew **5**:44). Love in its highest 'agape' form has been revealed in the Lord Jesus Christ.

John writes that 'God is [agape] love' (1 John **4**:8) but he is not thereby saying that love is all that God is. Rather, this statement is a message addressed to believers (as, of course, all the epistles are); the context is relational – the relationship between the believer and God – and has to do with believing, and confessing Jesus, and abiding in him. It is made clear that the love of which God is the perfect source is to be reflected in the lives of his people. (1 John **4**:8–21.)

The way each of the persons of the Holy Trinity relates to the other two persons is love, so love is in the godhead. We take from this great truth that it was not loneliness that prompted God to create human beings in his image, rather it was his will to share his perfect love with others. This helps us to define the nature of love in its purest form. It is 'my best for another's best'. Agape love which should exist amongst believers towards each other, instead of being self-centred, is focused on the welfare of another person. This kind of loving is truly godly for it reflects something of the very nature of God himself. It also follows that failure to love like this is to fall short of the glory of God: it is sin (Romans **3**:23). At the Fall, Adam and Eve put themselves at the centre instead of God and became tainted with sin (disobedience to God). The devil tempted them to sin; that sinfulness has been passed on to all of us (Romans **3**:10–18). Thus there was a gulf between man and God to deal with, and only God could provide what we need. When Jesus Christ came into the world and gave his life as the sacrifice for our sin, that was agape love. Jesus, true God and true man, opened up the only way for man to have the righteousness without which it is impossible to relate to a perfectly holy God.

God shows his love for us in that: 'While we were still sinners, Christ died for us' (see Romans **5**:8). Jesus always put his Father first, and could say: "Whoever has seen me has seen the Father" (see John **14**:8–11). Perfect love shows the character of Christ (see Ephesians **3**:19). Love includes: praying for enemies, as we have seen, and putting the Lord first (see Matthew **10**:37). It is patient, kind, and not envious, boastful, arrogant, rude, self-seeking, irritable, resentful (bearing grudges), and it is not glad when there is wrongdoing. Love is long-suffering, eager to believe the best, hopes in all circumstances, endures no matter what happens, and never comes to an end. (See 1 Corinthians **13**:4–8). Love banishes fear (1 John **4**:18), and does no wrong to a neighbour (Romans **13**:10). Love delights in serving (Galatians **5**:13). It is not worldly (see 1 John **2**:15–17).

We cannot do all this in our *own* strength, for in our natural, fallen state we all tend to put ourselves and our interests before the good of others. Our own efforts are inadequate. Spiritual giftedness is no substitute for it (1 Corinthians **12**:31–**13**:3); good works are no substitute for it (1 Corinthians **13**:3; Titus **3**:5); even a martyr's death is no substitute for it (1 Corinthians **13**:3).

Godly love is of God and must be God's own doing in us through the Holy Spirit (Galatians **5**:22–23). All need to be 'born again' of water and Spirit. We can then be aware of Christ in [us], 'the hope of glory' (see Colossians **1**:27). The way of life and love is made available to sinners who repent and believe in the Lord Jesus Christ, who are baptised in Holy Spirit and go on being filled with the Holy Spirit. It is the calling of those who belong to Christ to live their lives in step with the Holy Spirit. As fruit grows unconsciously upon the branches of a tree, so agape love will grow and appear unconsciously in the personality of believers, as the Spirit works in their lives and they co-operate in that life. Fruit could not survive if it were only tied onto branches! In the same way, this genuinely Christlike life of true love springs from regeneration – though, after regeneration, much sanctification and reforming of thinking has still to occur as we let our minds be renewed by God's word!

John **3**:6–21; **13**:35; **15**:1–5; Romans **5**:5; **8**:35–39; Ephesians **2**:4–6, **5**:2; Philippians **2**:12–13; 2 Timothy **1**:13; 2 Peter **1**:3–11; **3**:18; 1 John **4**:7–8, 16.

Love in the fellowship: a truly New Testament perspective

We have said a good deal about the life of agape love that must mark the life of believers – and an extremely important point to note is that this is **corporate** as well as personal. Many commands of Jesus in the Gospels, as well as the teachings of the apostles in their letters, are *addressed to believers about relating to each other*. These instructions are to shape the life of churches (fellowships of Christians) teaching them about how brothers and sisters in Christ are to behave with one another. This is a salutary message, and often a dimension of New Testament teaching rather unfamiliar to believers today, who may be less aware of the corporate aspect of the fellowship of disciples in an individualistic age and culture. The New Testament teaching about love applies to every disciple of Jesus today personally, and to every group of Christians who meet together too.

Our agape love toward God: an essential that is easy to miss!

We have considered *God's agape love* expressed in the single act in which he once gave his only-begotten Son as the perfect sacrifice for our sin so that we might not perish but instead have eternal life. We have also considered the agape love that believers in the fellowship are to have for each other. But there is another vital kind of agape love that disciples are to have: **the agape love of the believer toward Jesus Christ**. Again, this is a dimension which is often missed, yet it is essential in the Christian Way. What exactly is *this* kind of agape love? It is obviously somewhat different from God's love toward us, for as we have seen he has provided for our greatest need in the person of his Son Jesus Christ. God himself has no 'need' that we could meet as he is perfect and he owns everything anyway! There is a popular misconception about what our love toward God is (or should be) like. There is a 'sentimental' view of the matter which says it is like being 'in love' with Jesus. However, that way of putting it is a usage in English which does not express the key that Jesus provided. Happily, Jesus did speak of the kind of love that every disciple is to have *toward God* and it is extremely simple – straightforward enough for even the most uneducated believer to understand and live out. Jesus said: "If you keep my commandments, you will abide in my [agape] love, just as I have kept my Father's commandments and abide in his love" (John **14**:10); and, "If you love [agape] me, keep my commandments" (John **14**:15). The message is clear: obedience is central. Moreover, it is a message directed to those who are already believers, so that they will continue, persevere, *abide* in (agape) love. They are not to fall into disobedience to God; they are not to wander away into a position of unbelief or to adopt immoral ways of behaving.

It is recommended that the Bible student should study chapters 14–17 of John's Gospel with these three questions in mind: What did Jesus say concerning the love God has towards the disciples, and about the love we are to have toward himself (Jesus), and about the love believers are to have toward each other? Such study will reveal that the love of God is very far from being 'unconditional', a word that does not appear in scripture but which is often heard nowadays! Jesus often says "If...." Note carefully the points at which he does so, in order to understand and minister the word of truth faithfully to others.

So what of John **3**:16, a verse considered by many to be the most important in the whole Bible, which includes the words '. . . for God so loved the world . . .' ? Once again, a problem arises in translation. The word often rendered 'so' means 'thus' and refers back to something else – the event referred to in John **3**:14 in fact! From v. 14 we learn that God gave his Son *thus – in the same way* as Moses lifted up the snake in the desert. The snake on the pole in that context was used by God to provide the way sinners could avoid the death sentence for the sin of grumbling, for which they were being punished in the desert. That was why they were being killed by the snakes, as a punishment for their sin. 'Thus' or 'so' indicates how Jesus being lifted up (on the cross) is, in the same way, the only means by which humans may have their sins forgiven and so be freed from the sentence of death that sin deserves.

People tend to think that John 3:16 means God *loves* (in a continuous sense) the world *so* much that he gave his Son. But it really means that God acted once in the sacrifice of Jesus (in agape love), and the past aorist Greek tense is used, signifying a one-time act of love (meeting a need in unworthy sinners whose sins deserve death). The one sacrifice was sufficient to meet anyone's need for forgiveness if they would go on believing in Jesus. It is a verse which, when properly understood, encourages the believer to go on believing and so to go on having eternal life. (See Note 2.)

It is also a verse that, if properly understood, may help the unsaved sinner to see that Jesus' once for all sacrifice can be their means of salvation, too.

Notes

[1]For a full treatment of this vital subject, refer to a good Bible encyclopedia. The Baker Encyclopedia of the Bible is highly recommended. Some of the comments above are indebted to that publication, but have been adapted.

[2] See David Pawson, *Is John 3:16 the Gospel?* (Terra Nova Publications, 2007).

26
THE TRUE CHURCH

A true believer and follower of Jesus is always called by God to relate closely to other such believers, whenever possible.

Forming communities of believers – where there can be a proper commitment to proclaiming the gospel, sound biblical teaching, prayer, praise, baptism, sharing Holy Communion (breaking of bread/Eucharist) and maintaining a loving fellowship in the power of the Holy Spirit – are vital aspects of the biblical understanding of what it is to be 'church'.

The word 'church' is the standard translation of the Greek word 'ecclesia' (literally 'called out'), used 112 times in the New Testament, but in some translations the terms 'congregation', 'meeting' or 'assembly' are used. The Greek word in James **2**:2 is not *'ecclesia'* but *'sunagoge'* (synagogue), a term with an especially rich history for Jews of course, tending to emphasise the significance of the 'assembly' of the believers, who gather together for corporate worship, prayer and teaching.

The Bible uses several illustrations to explore the meaning of the church.

1. The Israelites were a chosen people and were rescued from Egypt (see Acts chapter 7); disciples of Jesus (the church) are rescued from slavery to sin.

2. A human body has different 'members' or parts, with many different functions. So does the church. (See 1 Corinthians **12**:12–27; Ephesians **5**:29–30.)

3. It is likened to a holy temple in which Jesus dwells. (See 1 Corinthians **3**:16–17; Ephesians **2**:21–22; 1 Peter **2**:5.)

4. It is like a bride in a true love marriage where Jesus himself is the husband. (See Ephesians **5**:28–30.)

5. It is like a virgin, betrothed to Jesus. (See Matthew **25**:1–13; 2 Corinthians **11**:2–3.)

The true church is the community of true believers in and followers of Jesus. This includes both those believers living today and those who have died. It is better to think of the church as a living organism rather than primarily in terms of institutions, buildings and organisations, though every particular 'church' (whether an individual congregation or a denomination) has some level of organisational structure and leadership. Seeking appropriate leadership is biblical and enables community life to flourish by making sure that all things are done 'decently and in order'. In the Christian creeds the term 'catholic' refers to the universal nature of the church (God's self-revelation in Jesus Christ, his claims and the gospel are true everywhere, and addressed to all people), and the term 'apostolic' refers to the fact that the church is built upon the faithful foundation of apostolic witness and teaching. Sadly, the one true 'universal' and 'apostolic' church in the world today is divided into numerous denominations and groupings. There are historical, theological and pragmatic reasons for this, but it does appear to go strongly against the will of Jesus for true unity amongst his disciples. (See John **17**:6–26.)

The fact is that when true Christian believers meet each other there can be a real awareness of unity in the Spirit, which transcends denominations, because it concerns a real fellowship, with a living relationship with the Lord Jesus Christ. Many testify to this experience, and it is not about legal, denominational structures. In God's ongoing purposes there is a clear link between unity and effective mission. The unity in the Spirit which is experienced by believers should not be confused with uniformity in external structures of organisation or styles of worship.

27

THE PRIESTHOOD

After the fall of mankind (Genesis 3), God provided a way of salvation and forgiveness in which each individual could find atonement for sin in anticipation of the perfect sacrifice for sin which Jesus would make by his death upon the cross. Therefore in the Bible we find examples of key people such as Abel, Noah and Abraham approaching God by sacrifice. Such sacrifice focused upon repentance, faith and the shedding of the blood of an animal. (See Hebrews **11**:4.)

Mankind is in rebellion against God and has been ever since the Fall. The image of God in each person is marred and tarnished by sin. All have sinned and fallen short of God's glory (Romans **3**:23). God chose to form a particular people – through the covenant with the patriarch Abraham (Genesis chapters 12, 15 and 17) and later through the covenants with Moses and David – to serve him and to point the way back to him. In a sense the whole Jewish nation became a nation of priests (Exodus **19**:5–6), yet to the tribe of Levi God gave particular priestly functions within firstly the tabernacle and, later, the Jerusalem temple.

In the fullness of God's time and salvation purposes, he sent his Son Jesus into the world (see John **3**:16, Romans **5**:6–11). Through the perfect life and obedient death of Jesus a complete and once-for-all sacrifice for sin was made. Jesus became sin for us, so that in him we might become the righteousness of God. (See 2 Corinthians **5**:21) The veil of the Holy of Holies in the temple was torn open (Matthew **27**:51) and a 'new and living way' was made, so all people can receive atonement for sin and be reconciled to God through Jesus.

Christians are called to offer their bodies as living sacrifices, holy and pleasing to God (Romans **12**:1). Christians are now a royal priesthood (1 Peter **2**:9) as they share in the benefits of Jesus' priestly ministry. (See Hebrews 10.)

The word 'priest' has two main meanings today. In the Bible the term predominantly comes from the Hebrew *kohen* or the Greek *hiereus*, and in the New Testament usage the term refers variously to Jewish temple priests, the Lord Jesus as high priest, or to Christians offering spiritual sacrifices. In some Church traditions and prayer books the Greek word *presbuteros* (probably best translated 'elder') is sometimes rendered as 'priest'. This is largely unhelpful as there is little connection between the New Testament 'elder' (church leader) and the Old Testament 'priest'.

See also Study No. 29 and references there to the false 'teaching of the Nicolaitans'. Also Study No. 30 on the subject of Sacerdotalism.

28
PRAYER

Prayer is a key feature of the Christian life. It has been said that prayer is 'the air which Christians breathe'. It is communication with God, and it has many aspects: listening, confession, thanksgiving and asking (intercession) for your needs and the needs of others. It can be spoken or silent, solitary or corporate. Even when praying on your own, in prayer you are not really alone because the persons of the Holy Trinity are involved (see below).You may well discover that you are engaged in a kind of spiritual warfare as you pray that God's will be done on earth.

Prayer implies a relationship with the living God, and it requires trust, love, and openness to the work of the Holy Spirit.

In the Old Testament there is a rich heritage of prayer especially based around God's covenantal faithfulness. See, for example, texts such as Genesis **18**:23–32; **32**:9–11; Exodus **32**:11–13; **33**:12–21; 1 Samuel **1**:10–11; 1 Kings **8**:23ff; Nehemiah **1**:5ff; Psalm **57**; Jonah **2**:2; **4**:2.

In the New Testament a new intimacy in prayer was modelled by Jesus, as he spoke and listened to his heavenly Father. His disciples were able to see his deep prayer life, and to learn from his teaching, as when he instructed them to pray personally to their Father, who knows their needs. (See Matthew **6**:5–15; **7**:7–12.) Following the outpouring of the Holy Spirit at Pentecost (recorded in Acts chapter 2), Christians are able to pray with the help of the Holy Spirit at work within them (see Romans **8**:26–28). This type of prayer becomes the bedrock for Christian life and mission (Romans **10**:1; 1 Thessalonians **3**:10; 1 Timothy **2**:8; Hebrews **13**:18–19; Jude v. 20). Faithful believers are living *in* Christ and that makes Christian prayer distinctive, giving it the particular intimacy to which we have referred. Prayer is the cry of the church. (See Revelation **22**:20b).

The Bible teaches us to pray to God as our Father, in the name of Jesus (this points to the truth that in prayer, as in all things, the Christian is to rely on who Jesus is and what he has accomplished), and in the power of the Holy Spirit. This also points to the Trinitarian understanding of God. The true, living God hears the cries of his people (Exodus **2**:23f) and he acts powerfully.

29
THE ROADS TO APOSTASY

Background

The word 'apostasy' derives from the Greek *apostasia* which means to 'withdraw' or to 'fall away' (2 Thessalonians **2**:3). Today it is used to mean the abandonment by a professing Christian of the fundamental principles of the Christian gospel. History shows that apostasy does not generally come into the church as a single event. Its encroachment is gradual and insidious. All Christians therefore need to be aware of the 'roads' that lead to apostasy, alert to the possibility of treading those roads themselves, and prepared to help others to see the danger. The short letter of Jude in the New Testament warns about this dreadful danger. The Holy Bible identifies at least three dangerous 'roads':

1. The 'way of Cain' (Jude 11), i.e. a 'bloodless' religion, that rejects in some way the full Bible teaching on the Cross;
2. The 'error of Balaam' (Jude 11), i.e. compromise with the world (see also Study 16 – *Separation* – in this regard);
3. The 'teaching of the Nicolaitans' – compromise with the world, but especially with other religions.

There are surely other paths that lead away from 'the Way' (Acts **24**:14, 22) but these three above seem to have beset Christ's church from the very beginning. We examine them in greater detail below:

The Way of Cain

This applies when a Christian seeks a way of forgiveness of his sins by any other means than cleansing through the blood of Jesus. The idea that we can be forgiven by our 'good works' is perhaps the most insidious and pervasive example; or, through the intellect, to believe that Jesus is an 'example' that we should strive to follow in our own strength, but not feel too disheartened when we fail! This is perhaps the key outcome of 'modernism' or 'liberalism' wherever it is encountered in the church of Christ – it certainly seems to have made real headway in the organised church in the twentieth century. An apparently opposed form of the error – that of Cain – is those religious people (and we have in mind here people within the Christian church) who may be trusting in their religious profession or their 'zeal' for God, whilst sin remains unsurrendered and uncleansed in their hearts. The zealot and the extreme liberal are often closer than either of them would like to admit!

If we understand the biblical account of Cain (Genesis 4) correctly, it seems that Cain found no peace with God, and then looked in anger at his brother whose sacrifice had been found acceptable to God. Anger can be a sign that sin remains uncleansed. Not only individuals, but also whole Christian communities can tread the 'way of Cain'. We think then of extreme liberal 'churches' with no vital message – or strictly orthodox ones, but often riven with internal dissension and jealousy.

Genesis **4**:1–5 (Hebrews **11**: 4); Acts **15**:1, 2, 19, 24; **20**:30; 2 Corinthians **11**:3; Galatians **1**:6–9; **2**:11–16; **3**:1–4; **6**:12–15; Philippians **3**:18, 19 (the perversion of the cross of Christ into a license for sin); Colossians **2**:16, 17, 20–23 (adding non-essentials to the gospel); 2 Timothy **4**:3–4; 2 Peter **2**:1–2; 14–15; 2 John **7**; Jude 3, 4 and 11.

The Way of Balaam

For the Christian this implies compromise with the world. (2 Peter **2**:15). It is clear from the account in the book of Numbers that this prophet-for-hire failed God in two ways:

He desired to make a market of his divine gift (Numbers **22**:12, 18, 19). Although in the end he reluctantly complied with God's commands (the right decision), he seemed to look for a change of heart in God that might bring him material rewards.

He taught the Israelites to defile themselves with heathen practices (Numbers **25**:1 – 3; **31**:16).

For the Christian disciple, Balaam's way represents any 'sharp practice' with money, or of making the Lord's service a way to worldly advancement or gain. It also represents worldliness, when the soul is no longer satisfied with the Lordship of Jesus, and so satisfaction from the world is sought. The result is a church infected by this worldly spirit, and accordingly resorting to worldly methods (e.g. raising money via lottery) or dependence on the arm of flesh (e.g. asking for State handouts so as to be able to perform 'good works'). At one extreme, parts of the church seem to think they are an extension of the social services. For a time such methods may appear to succeed, but there is an inevitable loss of spiritual vitality and an increasing deadness in ministry.

Matthew **7**:15; Luke **16**:13; 2 Corinthians **11**:13–15; 1 Timothy **6**:5, 10; 2 Timothy **3**:5; 2 Peter **2**:17, 20–21; Jude 11, 16.

The Teaching of the Nicolaitans

The Nicolaitans were a heretical sect of the very early church mentioned twice in the book of Revelation. (Revelation **2**:6, 15). Amongst some 'Christian' sects is found 'priestcraft' and religious domination in different ways. This is an intrusion of a man-made priesthood. Jesus the Christ is our high priest and has opened up a way for all believers that is independent of any human agency. At its worst, this priestcraft tries to divide the body of Christ into priests and laity, and to put the 'priests' into the position of mediators between man and God. The effect is that both 'priest' and people tend to lose faith in Christ alone and instead put their faith in ceremonial and outward forms. There are many warnings of this and it does seem that in the end times, an apostate 'Christendom' will be reunited under one supreme head (and possibly united with other religions). The Bible calls this person *the* antichrist as he will set himself up as a Messiah of some sort.

Priestly domination seems to lead invariably to religious persecution.

Isaiah **1**:4–6; 13–15; **5**:5–7; Ezekiel **8**:9–16 (idolatry in the House of the Lord); Colossians **2**:20–23; 1 Timothy **2**:5; **4**:1–3.

In Conclusion

Believers in the true Messiah, Jesus, are to be alert to the temptation from our enemy to turn away from the salvation journey on which we are embarked. The warnings are sufficiently frequent, both in the Old and the New Testaments, that we cannot avoid the conclusion that we are being given *real and urgent* warnings. It would be foolish to ignore these. The illusion of self-earned salvation, the temptations of the world, and the imposition of false religiousness are each real and dangerous errors to avoid. Christians should prayerfully be aware of these, on the watch for them, and gently seek to help others who may be in danger of falling into them.

30

SACERDOTALISM –
AND GOD'S ANSWER TO IT

Background

'Sacerdotalism' is not a word we use every day! This is an area of controversy of which the diligent Bible student needs to be aware. At its most basic, it has to do with the imposition of 'priest' between God and people. It is a key understanding of Christianity that, at exactly the same time as Jesus died on the cross, the veil in the Jerusalem Temple was torn from top to bottom. Hitherto only the High Priest could pass through it in order to enter the Holy of Holies. So in the sight of all the world God had opened up the way, removing the barrier. God has now raised up a priesthood of all believers (see 1 Peter **2**:9; Revelation **5**:10). All believers can enter into the Holy of Holies as children of God.

The Priesthood of All Believers

The first century church had no priests, and the New Testament nowhere uses this word to describe those in church leadership, but the idea of a 'priesthood' began to emerge forcefully again in the third century AD. The biblical concept of God's priesthood being all believers is revealed in different ways throughout the Bible. (See Exodus **19**:6; Psalm **50**:23; Psalm **51**:17-19; Psalm **141**:2; Hebrews **13**:10–16; 1 Peter **2**:5–9).

Aspects of Sacerdotalism

The list below is not exhaustive, but indicates the key dimensions of sacerdotalism.

1. *Denial of grace*

(a) Salvation by works (Galatians **1**:8–9; **2**:16; Titus **3**:5).

(b) Self-mortifications, penances, etc. (Colossians **2**:16–23; 1 Timothy **4**:3).

(c) Celibacy as a *requirement* for ministry or a supposedly higher 'religious' life (1 Timothy **3**:2; 12; **4**:3–4). All the apostles except Paul were married men, Peter being especially mentioned. (See 1 Corinthians **9**:5). The celibacy of Paul indicates that it can be an appropriate condition for some people.

(d) Monastic communities have sometimes been founded to reform the church, providing help to the needy, but historically they have sometimes departed from principles of gospel living. (See Galatians **5**:1).

(e) The doctrine of purgatory (Luke **23**:42 – 43; 1 John **1**:7– 9; the blood cleanses, not further work or punishment).

Sacerdotalism tends to promote the false (and proud) view that we can 'earn' some aspect of our salvation. Man's pride constantly resists the idea that only Jesus has achieved the conditions for our forgiveness and acceptance. He alone lived the absolutely sinless life. (To point this out is not to deny that we are to co-operate with him as the Spirit changes us; throughout our lives as Christians we *are* to live holy lives and grow in obedience to the Lord. How easy it is, though, to begin to credit ourselves for supposedly meritorious acts or privations which are not even part of the 'law of Christ', and congratulating ourselves rather than giving all the glory to God!)

2. *Love of splendour and the praise of men*

Too much in what is pleased to call itself 'church' is bound up with outward show – and apparent inward barrenness. (See Matthew **23**:5–12; Luke **22**:25–26; 1 Timothy **6**:3–10; 1 Peter **5**:1–3.)

3. *Ignorance*

Fear of, and blind obedience to 'priests' or even to church 'elders'. Such deference tends to keep us in ignorance, and sadly that is where some desire to remain! (See Matthew **15**:13–14; Romans **8**:15; Jude 12–13.)

4. *False worship*

Some worship the bread and wine in the communion or eucharist. (Hebrews **7**:27; **9**:12; **9**:25–28). Some worship crucifixes, saints, relics, and Mary the mother of Jesus (Exodus **20**:3–5; **32**:4; Psalm **115**:4–8; Isaiah **44**:14–20; Revelation **19**:10; **22**:8–9).

5. *Hindering of the realisation of salvation being available to all who repent, believe in and trust Jesus*

Some teach that salvation is found only within their own sect. Others teach apostolic succession only through their own priesthood. Yet others use language not understood by the ordinary people or make access to the Holy Scriptures difficult. All these things hinder the understanding that salvation is freely available to those who repent before God, put their trust and faith in Jesus and are baptised. (Matthew **11**:28; **23**:13; **28**:19–20; Acts **2**:38–41.)

6. *The practice of the use of intermediaries*

The imposition of 'priests' can open the door to apostasy in individual believers as well as whole communities of believers: there is the so-called infallibility of popes, even where their teaching contradicts Scripture, for example, (Mark **7**:9–13); priestly or ritualistic 'pardons' (Romans **5**:1–2; Hebrews **10**:19; 1 John **1**:7–9); and invocation of 'saints' as intermediaries. (Matthew **11**:28; John **6**:37; Acts **4**:12 – note that Peter is the speaker; Ephesians **3**:12.) We are to approach God the Father through Jesus his Son – not through anyone else.

7. *False prayers*

The encouragement of long-winded repetitions; ostentatious prayer in public; prayers for the dead. Matthew **6**:5–7; Mark **12**:40.

8. *False ritual*

The beautiful simplicity of the gospel can be obscured by rites, ceremonial and observances. Ritualism can be all about outward performances rather than faith in Jesus Christ and true, personal worship of God. (Matthew **15**:9; Colossians **2**:16.)

9. Sin – and how Sacerdotalism can mislead

To understand what can go wrong in a 'sacerdotal' approach, we first have to recap and summarise some key points about sin and forgiveness. The Bible does make some distinctions between different kinds of sin. Under the Mosaic covenant, punishments varied (cf. Deuteronomy chapter 17 and chapter 22). However, it is made clear that *all* sin separates man from God, and that man's fallen condition (or 'original sin') is at the root of particular sins. When we repent of our sin and believe in Jesus and are baptised into him in water and Spirit, we have been saved from the penalty of sins committed up to that point, and we have begun a new life in him. The New Testament makes it perfectly clear that believers need to *continue* believing in Jesus and to repent of sins committed *after* conversion (see 1 John 1:8–10, addressed to believers). The believer has been saved from the penalty of death for past sin, but is still *being saved* from the *power* of sin – but now with the help and presence of the Holy Spirit.

There are distinctions to be made at this point: there is sin that leads to death and that which does not (see 1 John 5:16). Moreover, the New Testament does indeed establish ethical and disciplinary procedures within the body of Christ. However, man's tendency to want to create religious rules has gone far beyond the principles established in Scripture, elaborating the minutiae of regulations and hence leading people to think that outward adherence to complex ethical systems is the heart of the matter. In fact the law of Christ often goes well beyond the requirements of the law of Moses (consider Jesus' extension of the meaning of 'adultery', for one example) and we are never to water down his teaching or become 'antinomian' (wrongly believing that we can be lawless or immoral in our behaviour; see the brief but extremely important Epistle of Jude, again written to Christians). But when the focus is *merely* on outward observance and performance, it is all too easy to fall into the trap of imagining that *by our own efforts* we have made ourselves holy and acceptable or are continuing to do so. In fact we are to give God the glory all the time. That applies in relation to our initial salvation from the penalty of sin (death) won for us by the sacrifice of the only one who was without sin, Jesus; and it applies too as we continue to repent of and receive forgiveness for many subsequent sins of thought, word and deed, action and neglect, in the course of our 'sanctification' throughout our Christian life – as we go on repenting and go on believing and seeking to obey his commands (see John **15**:10) and go on abiding in him (as, again, he taught disciples to do; see John **15**:1–8).

The Bible student does well to read the epistles again, looking at the dynamic way in which the apostolic writers characterised this ongoing Christian life in terms of a fight and a race. The main focus should be on what Jesus himself taught about the eternal consequences of sin. Then, whenever we are forgiven, we will have a right understanding of what he has won for us. Sacerdotalism, however, tends to put the focus on *us* and our imagined achievements in terms of detailed observances of ecclesiastical rules, lists and elaborations, rather than on Jesus and an inward heart of faithfulness and obedience to him. (See Matthew **5**:20–23; **23**:16–22; James **2**:10.)

Conclusion

Sacerdotalism, or reliance upon 'priests' (howsoever they identify themselves), is controversial and this is a controversy that cannot be avoided by the diligent seeker after truth. Anyone who seeks to put themselves between man and God (by becoming a spiritual 'father figure') seeks to take away some of the glory of Jesus – it is as serious as that. This is not to say that a maturer Christian cannot offer wise counsel and be a prayer partner, helping a younger Christian to grow. But sacerdotalism goes far beyond that useful and godly help. It creates barriers for seekers after truth. We need to heed Jesus' warning in Matthew **23**:9.

31

BAPTISM

The word 'baptism' comes from the Greek word *baptizo*, meaning to dip, plunge or cleanse in water. The word was commonly used to describe the process of dyeing cloth. The word in the New Testament is used to describe cleansing things as well as baptising persons. (See Mark **7**:4.) In Christian teaching and practice, baptism involves testifying before others to faith and trust in Jesus Christ, and is the sign of cleansing from sin.

In the Old Testament period there were some ceremonial practices of ritual washing and purification. (See Exodus **29**:4, Numbers **19**:13.) The New Testament records, firstly, the kind of baptism administered by John the Baptist. He baptised and he heard God's command (John **1**:33). John was calling out to a largely disobedient people to repent and to prepare for the coming Messiah (the Messiah who would baptise with the Holy Spirit and fire; see Luke **3**:16.)

The exact relationship between Jewish ritual washing (a practice which continues today in rabbinical Judaism and is referred to as the practice of *Mikveh*), the baptism of John and Christian baptism, is an area of much debate.

At the heart of Christian baptism is the fact that it is carried out in the name of God, Father, Son and Holy Spirit (as part of the great commission; see Matthew **28**:19b). Baptism involves public testimony of the decision that has been made to **repent** and **believe** in Jesus Christ. (Recall the preaching of Peter on the day of Pentecost; Acts **2**:28). It is an outward sign of an inner reality. Baptism also marks entry into the life of the church community. It is described in terms of a death to sin and there is a very important link with the death of Jesus. (See Romans **6**:4; we were buried with him through baptism so that as he was raised from the dead we may live a new life.) There is a celebration of the new life and hope Jesus brings to his people through his death, resurrection and ascension. The act of baptism is often referred to as a Christian sacrament (along with Holy Communion/The Lord's Supper). A sacrament is understood to be an outward sign which points to what is happening through the grace of God.

Most Christians agree that Jesus himself ordained baptism as a sign of the new covenant (again, see Matthew **28**:19f), and that it is therefore a central part of becoming a Christian, along with faith, repentance, and baptism in the Holy Spirit. (See Acts **2**:38; **8**:6–38; **10**:44–48; Colossians **2**:12). Clearly there are exceptions when baptism is not possible (consider the thief dying on a cross; Luke **23**:43) but baptism should be part of the 'normal process' of Christian initiation, as it clearly was in New Testament times. [It must be recorded that a very small minority of Christians do not consider baptism essential.]

Nowadays, baptism is usually carried out by recognised leaders of the church, though there is no New Testament rule laid down as to who administers it. The method of baptism varies in different church traditions, yet from the point of view of adherence to what was normative in the early church, it is suggested that total immersion in the water is implied by the Greek term.

There is debate within the church about the appropriateness of baptising infants. Many churches practise infant baptism, believing that the children of Christians should be baptised with the expectation that later they will own and accept for themselves what that baptism claims (on coming to personal repentance/faith/trust in Jesus). However, other churches believe that the weight of the biblical teaching on baptism clearly shows that baptism demands the repentance and faith of the candidate *before* their baptism. It is therefore taught that baptism should only be for believers (although there is debate about what is the youngest possible age a person can freely confess their own faith), while infants should be welcomed into the church community by a ceremony of blessing/dedication but not by way of the (once-only) act of baptism.

32

THE LORD'S SUPPER

The Lord's Supper is known in various church traditions by other names, such as 'Holy Communion', the 'Breaking of Bread' and the 'Eucharist' (from the Greek, meaning 'thanksgiving'). This act (often known as a 'sacrament'; see Unit 31, *Baptism*) takes place frequently in churches, in obedience to the command of Jesus to his disciples at his last supper before he was crucified.

Jesus, a Jew, shared in the religious life of the Jewish community which included the celebrating of the three pilgrim festivals (Passover, Pentecost and Tabernacles) in Jerusalem. The final meal Jesus shared with his disciples before his crucifixion is identified as a Passover meal (see Luke **22**:15; Mark **14**:14; Matthew **26**:18). The Passover was a time of celebration and re-dedication, primarily in a family setting. The Passover involved looking back, remembering God's great act of liberating his people from slavery in Egypt. (See Exodus **12**:3–13; Exodus **13**:8; Deuteronomy **16**:1–8; 2 Chronicles **30**; Ezekiel **45**:21).

The Passover meal and readings focus upon liberation and freedom. Jesus himself draws out the fuller meaning of these terms by speaking of the liberation his death and resurrection would bring. Jesus is the Passover lamb (1 Corinthians **5**:7) and by his sacrifice we have been (and are being) made holy (see Hebrews **10**:10–14; 1 Peter **1**:17–22). Jesus brings new meaning to eating the Passover bread and drinking the wine (John **6**:53; Luke **22**:17–20). It is a spiritual feeding, an act of sharing, celebrating and remembering.

To feed on the body of Jesus broken for us and his blood shed for us is to take to ourselves in faith and thankfulness the victory of his death and resurrection. It is an act of public discipleship in which we seek to enter into a closer unity with Jesus and with those who share with us in the life of the Church. The outward actions of eating the bread and drinking the wine are pictures (symbols) of the inward action of feeding on what the bread and wine represents. The outward act of eating has no spiritual significance apart from the inward act of feeding on Jesus (who is present with his people; see Matthew **18**:20) with the heart.

As with the teaching on baptism, churches have differing traditions as to the method, style and frequency of sharing the Lord's Supper. There is no direct teaching from the New Testament concerning who should preside, nor specifying the place or precise timing of the Lord's Supper, although today most churches have their own normative patterns. Some, for example, would suggest that the celebration of the Lord's Supper should take place at each major (weekly) Christian worship gathering (Acts **20**:7), while at the other extreme some would suggest it should take the form of an annual sharing (linked to Passover). For some the Lord's Supper should be an informal sharing; the Breaking of Bread often takes place in home groups. That has a particular resonance with early church practice before Christianity was adopted as the state religion of the Roman empire; and small group settings can also be helpful today (notably, for practical reasons, wherever there is persecution of believers). The term 'Breaking of Bread' (probably the earliest name for the Lord's Supper) suggests an informal custom at the close of a common fellowship meal. In some traditions the pattern becomes more elaborate and structured. Whatever the outward forms, the heart of the matter is to obey the command of Jesus (1 Corinthians **11**:24). By remembering Jesus in the way he ordained we honour him and we open our lives afresh to his power and grace. We celebrate his death (he has died), proclaim his resurrection and presence today (he is risen) and look joyfully to his future coming (he will come again).

It is worth noting that the custom of most churches has been to include some particular features in the meeting (or service) at which the actual breaking of bread takes place. From early times it was customary to include thanksgiving for all God's gifts in creation, as well as mention of the mighty acts of God in redemption through Jesus Christ; there is prayer and the reading of Scripture; usually the words Jesus used at the Last Supper with his disciples are spoken or mentioned. Most churches include an opportunity for repentance, which is significant, reminding us that the New Testament warns of dangers attending impenitent reception of the bread and wine, and the need for self-examination before eating and drinking at the Supper (see 1 Corinthians **11**:27–31). Many churches include in their prayers an invocation of the Holy Spirit.

Practical issues have arisen in the history of the church, especially in times of plague, concerning the use of a 'common cup' for communion, a practice which was revived in the Reformation period. Concerns about communicable diseases being passed by infected saliva on a shared cup have been expressed, and some churches have addressed this matter, allaying concerns, by using 'intinction', a method of putting a drop of wine on each piece of bread.

It is of interest that some churches use unleavened bread, reminding members of the Passover.

33

THE MISSIONARY CALL

The call to mission is not optional! It came from Jesus himself, and it is to and for every disciple. He instructed believers to go and make disciples of all the 'nations' (the Greek word used, '*ethne*', signifies: of all ethnic groups), baptising them and teaching them to observe all the things he had commanded. (See Matthew **28**:19–20.) Quite often, new believers discover early on in their new life in Christ a strong desire to tell others what God has done for them through the death and resurrection of Jesus. This sense of 'mission' should grow, not diminish! If Christians mature (as the Lord intends) and become 'more like Jesus', the awareness of that call from their Lord should grow stronger, not weaker; there should be a continuing willingness to be sent out to serve, to witness and, above all, to tell others the gospel and make disciples. (Being 'sent out' may not always mean being sent to a different location, though it sometimes does). The words of Jesus "*Peace be with you! As my Father sent me, I am sending you*" (John **20**:21) begin to challenge, and to shape the vision of Christians, who are to fulfil God's plan that all should hear the good news.

It should be emphasised that *every* Christian is to be a witness to the person and work of Jesus. The words of Peter (1 Peter **3**:15–16) give a wonderful sense of purpose to every Christian. Regardless of status, age, location and gifting, each has this calling. It does not in any way run counter to that call to all believers that some have specific callings from God to serve in special ways. Paul lists five ministries in Ephesians **4**:11 for which Jesus calls and equips particular Christians. In addition, Paul speaks of overseers/elders and deacons in his letters to Timothy and Titus. Paul also sets out the 'qualifications' and requirements for such ministries.

(See, for example, 1 Timothy chapter **3** and Titus **1**:5–9).

At the heart of hearing God's call to us must be an openness and willingness to obey, alongside the ability to discern needs and opportunities in order to reach out in Jesus' name. Such openness and willingness is reflected in the calling of many within the Bible. However, there is often a struggle in coming to terms with God's call – for example, Moses (Exodus **2**:12), Isaiah (Isaiah **6**:1–8), and Jeremiah (Jeremiah **1**:6). The key is that the God who calls is the God who equips. All God's people are being prepared for works of service (Ephesians **4**:12), each is encouraged to live a sacrificial life (Romans **12**:1–2) and to be open to the gifting of the Holy Spirit (1 Corinthians chapters **12–14**) as well as using our 'natural' abilities and resources in God's work.

In seeking to respond to God's call, it is important to try and examine our motives for doing so. Sometimes, sadly, our motives (to please people, pride, fame, need for affirmation, etc.) can distort what we do.

In the person of Jesus, in his earthly ministry, we see the perfect example of responding to the call of God. Jesus ministered in the power of the Holy Spirit. He reached out in compassion. His focus was always upon his Father's will (Matthew **26**:39) which he always obeyed perfectly. He spoke the truth fearlessly. He rebuked those who had hardened their hearts and had rejected the truth (especially the hypocritical who used 'religion' as a cloak); he taught those who came to him genuinely seeking the truth. He taught faith in very practical ways; he proclaimed the kingdom (power and authority) of God. He healed the sick and delivered those affected by demons. With self-evident authority he taught his disciples to do things he had shown them. He was obedient even unto death, and he warned believers that they would suffer for their faith in him, yet he promised that he would be with them always.

It was at Pentecost that the promised Holy Spirit came upon the disciples, who had already witnessed that Jesus had been raised from the dead, and the Spirit empowered them to fulfil the mission they had been given. The Holy Spirit has been empowering believers ever since, to go on witnessing in mission. Their message today is the same as it was for that first generation of disciples: it is good news which includes a call to repentance, and which proclaims the saving death and resurrection of Jesus, and it teaches of a righteousness that comes through faith, which will bear good fruit. The mission of the body of Christian believers includes both proclamation and teaching: both are necessary to make disciples who are to be in the 'Way', who will persevere and overcome and go on believing and trusting and obeying their Lord, no matter what challenges they may face.

34

THE PROBLEM OF SUFFERING

Background

Suffering, pain and trouble were among the results of man's original sin: the Fall. The world became disordered because mankind disobeyed the Creator. (See Genesis **1**:31; **2**:16–17; **3**:16–19.)

Some pain we might call 'suffering' serves a useful purpose. For example, if heat did not lead us to flinch from a hot surface we might be burned. But much human pain and suffering appears to be rather random. So believers are sometimes asked why God permits such suffering, whether at the hands of other people or as a result of events in nature such as earthquakes and tsunamis. Of course, Christians themselves are not immune to suffering – whether caused by natural disasters, sickness or direct human agency (as when people commit violent acts against others).

Basic beliefs about how God acts

There is a division between those who believe that God's relation to the universe is essentially that he set it all in motion and then left it to carry on without his direct intervention (a view called 'Deism'), and those who hold to the biblical perspective: that God not only created the world (all things, the universe), he also holds it in existence and he does intervene because he is actively in charge and, as scripture attests, he does miracles which glorify him.

The righteousness of God and the sinfulness of mankind

The puzzling question the unbeliever may ask as to *why God allows suffering* is best answered by looking at a characteristic of God: he is perfectly just, righteous, fair. The Bible witnesses to this at many points. The Bible student can search the prophetic books and discover a great many passages that reveal this. Jesus himself taught disciples about judgement, the punishment of the wicked in hell and the vindication of the righteous. The epistles and the book of Revelation attest to the coming righteous judgement.

So some suffering of mankind can be deserved, or may have a purpose in the divine plan; and, if some suffering is undeserved, we can be assured that God will right all injustices ultimately. Sinners will be punished in hell following an utterly just judgement. Wrongs will be righted at last. We might think that this will be wonderful: all the very bad people won't have got away with their evil deeds, and how good that will be for the rest of us! The problem with such thinking is that it means we are regarding ourselves as inherently, naturally good and deserving of divine approval. As has been indicated in other Units, the epistles (not least the opening chapters of Romans) spell out clearly the witness that runs right through the whole of scripture: sin is man's *natural* condition. Therefore all deserve to be punished by a good God, because we have *all* sinned. Only Jesus lived a perfect life. We have too high a view of man's goodness. We need to see the human race as God sees us: a race of fallen, disobedient, rebellious sinners. It is only because God is graciously giving mankind opportunities to repent and live righteously that we are being spared. That is not a right, it is a mercy.

Genesis **18**:25; Psalm **100**:5; **103**:1–14; **119**:67, 71, 75; Isaiah **59**:1–21

Corporate effects: people harm each other

In one sense, the 'problem' of suffering becomes less acute when we are aware of the sin operating among us. We can begin to see why things are as they are. Nonetheless, simple compassion makes us recoil at the suffering, for example, of sick or injured small babies who are too young to have committed deliberate sins. Then we come up against the fact that sinful human beings not only harm themselves, they harm others, and a climate of sin exists on earth in which those who are not personally directly culpable for a specific wrong are nonetheless getting hurt. There is a corporate dimension to man's disobedience which is hard for many people to understand because we tend to be individualistic in our thinking. (See Psalm **10**:1–11.)

God entered our suffering world . . . .

God may allow some suffering. Mankind has a measure of freedom to reject God's will and ways, and disobedience has consequences, some of which may occur in this life. Indeed, God can even use suffering for a good purpose. The formation of virtuous character and spiritual development may be energised by some suffering. God's good purposes might not always be understandable to the sufferer. (Job was unaware of some of the events described in chapters 1–2 of the Book of Job), but we can trust the Lord always to do right. In Christ, God himself has entered into our suffering. Jesus has taken sin and its punishment onto himself on the Cross so that there can be salvation and healing as foretastes of a final day of reckoning, the righting of wrongs and dealing with death.

Job **37**:13; **40**:1–8; Isaiah **25**:6–8; **53**:3–5; **55**:9; Matthew **10**:29–30; **13**:41–43; **25**:31–46; Mark **10**:18; Luke **13**:1–5, 22–30; John **4**:38–41; **9**:1–3; Acts **3**:1-8, **9**:36–42; Romans **8**:20–23; **8**:28–30; 1 Corinthians **2**:16; **15**:21–26; 2 Corinthians **1**:3–4; 1 Timothy **5**:23; 2 Timothy **4**:20; Hebrews **4**:16; **12**:5–11; James **1**:2–4; **5**:13–16; 1 Peter **1**:6–7; Revelation **21**:1–4

How can Christians deal with personal suffering?

So Christians face suffering with faith, enduring even when they cannot fathom all the whys and wherefores, drawing strength from the Lord, accepting that suffering may even spring from their loyalty to Christ. (Jesus warned disciples that in this world they would have trouble; John **16**:33.) We believe that God may choose to heal and deliver us even now, in his good purposes. We look to the Lord to bring good even in the midst of the suffering he permits. The faithful take courage from the knowledge that God will ultimately wipe away every tear. So, for a believer, suffering is only a passing problem: one day we shall share in the full salvation won for us at Calvary. Those who persevere in faith will triumph!

Genesis **45**:5–8; **50**:19–21; Job **1**:21–22; **5**:7; **23**:10; Psalm **9**:9; **27**:5; **91**:15, **94**:12; **121**:1–8; Isaiah **35**:10; **50**:10; Matthew **5**:11–12; **8**:16, **10**:8; Mark **16**:17–18; John **10**:27–29; **11**:25–26; **14**:1–3, 27; **15**:18–21; **16**:33; Acts **14**:22; Romans **5**:3–5; **8**:28–30; 1 Corinthians **12**:9; 2 Corinthians **4**:17; **7**:10; **12**:7–10; 1 Thessalonians **3**:2–4; 2 Thessalonians **1**:4–9; 2 Timothy **3**:11–12; Hebrews **11**:34–39; **12**:6–13; **13**:5–6; James **1**:2–3, 12; **5**:14–15; 1 Peter **1**:6–7; **2**:20–24; **3**:14–17; **4**:12–19; **5**:10; 2 Peter **2**:9; Jude 24–25; Revelation **1**:17–18; **3**:12; **21**:4

35

HEALING

Background

The whole matter of healing is bound up with the problem of sin. That must not be said in an accusatory way. It cannot be assumed that a person is ill and in need of healing because of any sin they might have committed. In John **9**:1–2 we learn that the disciples thought (incorrectly) that what they imagined to be the sin of a man or his parents was the cause of his blindness. Jesus corrected them. Neither the man nor his parents had sinned in that case. Elsewhere in Scripture the forgiveness of sins may be linked with healing ministry, either explicitly in the case of a paralytic (see Mark **2**:5) or *conditionally* – therefore *possibly* in some other cases (see James **5**:13–15).

The connection between sin and suffering (including sickness) originated at the Fall. In this fallen, suffering world, there is much sickness because of the general sinfulness of mankind. What people do and say affects others. In a simple, physical sense, it is easy to see how this can happen. If people act in ways that fail to show true love (care for others), and instead are motivated largely by greed and selfishness, then the health and wellbeing of people often suffers as a result, with environmental pollution, malnutrition and preventable diseases taking their toll.

So some sickness is caused in obvious and direct ways by the sins of others or the generally sinful attitudes and actions of mankind. But, as we have seen, in at least one case Jesus denied the existence of a link between an individual's own (supposed) sin and the bodily disorder concerned.

Some have suggested that sin is itself a 'sickness' but it

would be far from easy to justify that claim from Scripture. A biblical distinction must be maintained between the sin and sickness, and the metaphorical usage can confuse the issue. Sin is culpable disobedience to the will of God, whether in thought, word or deed. Sickness itself, however, is not something culpable (i.e. deserving of divine punishment) and not something which (in itself) needs forgiving. This is not to deny that the immediate causal factor in some disorders may sometimes have sinful antecedents (such as ungodly or disobedient lifestyles) which require repentance and divine forgiveness.

God has graciously given us a variety of ways to deal with the sicknesses that beset us. In biblical times, physicians like Luke (see Colossians 4:14) would have known about natural remedies. God has given us the ability to learn and understand a great deal about how our bodies function, what they need to thrive and how illnesses can be treated. So using medicine for healing is not somehow 'unspiritual'.

But from the very beginning of the ministry of Jesus on earth, his disciples have been given access to resources beyond the natural. Living personal faith in the Lord Jesus Christ, obedience to his commission to heal the sick, and the guidance and gifts of the Holy Spirit make the difference. We remember that healing is always God's gracious gift and never our 'right'.

In the Old Testament God sometimes granted miraculous healing and even life to the dead

Numbers 12:10, 13–15; 1 Kings 17:21–23; 2 Kings 4:32–36; 5:10–14; 20:7; Psalm 103:3; 116:3–9; 147:3; Isaiah 38:1–5

Jesus Christ came to bring healing and salvation

He applied Isaiah's prophecy to himself: *"The Spirit of the Lord is upon me, because he has anointed me to proclaim… liberty to the captives and recovery of sight to the blind, to set at liberty those who are oppressed, to proclaim the year of the Lord's favour"* (Luke **4**:18–19). He went about preaching and healing in the power of the Spirit, and told his disciples to preach and heal. The Christian attitude to suffering is given to us in the Parable of the Good Samaritan.

Isaiah **53**:5; **61**:1–2; Matthew **4**:23; **8**:7, 14–17; **9**:18–30; **10**:1, 7–8; **12**:15; **14**:14; Luke **4**:16–21; **7**:11–17; **10**:17–20, 25–37; John **11**:1–44

After Pentecost

In the life of the post-Pentecost church, healing was (and is) shown to be one of the gifts of the Holy Spirit. Yet there is a mystery here, for healing was not depicted as an *automatic right* in the life of the early church. Paul left Trophimus unwell in Miletus (2 Timothy **4**:20), told Timothy to drink wine for the sake of his stomach and his frequent ailments (see 1 Timothy **5**:23), and was relieved when Epaphroditus recovered remarkably after being so near to death (Philippians **2**:25–28). We are to pray in faith, and so we should be expectant even when we do not see immediate healing. The personal testimony of many Christians bears this out. We should believe that the Lord does indeed heal today, whether by medical or supernatural means. And we are to glorify him and thank him.

But Christians should not expect complete immunity to disease. As we have mentioned, we live in an environment (physical and social) which is often not conducive to good health. Nor should they be like those whom Christ rebuked because of their 'little faith', when healing of a boy with seizures was needed and the disciples could not heal the child (see Matthew **17**:15–21).

Medicine and the gospel

Medical clinicians may be used by the Lord to promote healing. This is God's common grace at work and does not necessarily make them Christian workers. Yet it truly expresses the compassionate nature of God when Christians are involved in both medical healing and the supernatural Christian ministry of healing the sick. It is still better when the gospel of righteousness is proclaimed (as many Christians have done in many cultures around the world) even as physical healing is administered. People need an opportunity to repent and to find forgiveness, as they come to the living, risen Lord Jesus Christ and believe in him alone.

We recall that Luke was both a physician *and* an evangelist. Healing miracles have been signs accompanying true Christian preaching from the time of the Acts of the Apostles.

Mark **16**:18; John **14**:12, 6–18; Acts **1**:8; **3**:6-8; **4**:22, 30; **5**:16; **9**:40–41; **28**:8–9; 1 Corinthians **12**:9, 28, 30; 2 Corinthians **12**:7–9 (cf. John **11**:4, 6, 14–15, 39–42); James **5**:13–18 (cf. 2 Chronicles **16**:12)

The kingdom

The believer receives joy and comfort from the knowledge that the Lord is one day going to eliminate all illness and suffering. Healing is a foretaste of heaven. It points to the Saviour whose kingdom is certain to come. In the meantime, the Christian trusts the Judge of all the earth to do what is right – whether we are in sickness or in health (Genesis **18**:25; cf. John **14**:1) – and we look continually to the coming King to show his power to save and heal broken lives.

Isaiah **25**:6–8; 1 Corinthians **15**:21–26; Revelation **21**:1–4

36
DOUBT

Background

There are many things that can creep in and cause doubt along the Christian way. Doubt can become a recurrent sin for individual Christians and will become a characteristic of the last days. Doubt causes coldness and a loss of spiritual vitality in those Christians who nurse doubts rather than working through them faithfully and prayerfully.

Finding things puzzling and having questions which we humbly ask the Lord is not condemned. Indeed, we are shown the disciples asking Jesus in order to learn from him, and he used such times to teach them. These sincere questions were very different in character from the mischievous questions which the Pharisees used to try to trick or ensnare Jesus. When we want to know something, we ask the Lord to show us and to guide us, and we ask in the context of a trusting, believing relationship with him, as disciples ask their Master to teach them.

Very different again is sceptical doubt that withdraws full commitment until there is absolute certainty. Such doubt undermines the Christian life, which depends on faith. Thinking "I have unsolved questions" is not the same as saying, "I will believe it when you prove it to me beyond doubt." Faith trusts the Lord Jesus to know the answers when we ourselves do not. In fact, He IS the answer. Christians trust a *person*, not a proof (even though there is good historical evidence, e.g. for the resurrection, and God sometimes graciously provides signs and wonders).

We note that there are many examples in the Bible of people who struggled with doubts

Abraham Genesis **17**:16–19, 21 with Romans **4**:18–22
Sarah Genesis **18**:9–15
Job (whose questionings are not answered directly):
Job **42**:1–6 (v. 6: "I despise [myself]" could equally be translated "I despise [what I have said]")
The sons of Korah Psalm **42**:5, 9–11
Asaph's wrestling with doubt Psalm **73**:1–22, **77**:7–9
Jeremiah Jeremiah **15**:18
The father of the boy with an unclean spirit Mark **9**:24
Peter Matthew **14**:28–33
Nathanael John **1**:46–47
Thomas John **20**:25
The Eleven Mark **16**:14
The circumcision party Acts **11**:2–3 [but see v. 18!]
The praying believers Acts **12**:12–16
Dietary doubters Romans **14**:23
Some of the 500 brothers 1 Corinthians **15**:6 with Matthew **28**:17
The waverer James **1**:6–8
Wobbling Christians Jude 22

If doubting thoughts present themselves to our minds from time to time, how are we to deal with them?

First of all, always remember that the Bible does not commend doubt. Whilst we are to be merciful to those who doubt (Jude 22), that does not mean that doubt itself is ever encouraged! The consistent scriptural encouragement is not to doubt but to believe (see again, for example, James **1**:6–8). In John 20, the Lord dealt kindly with Thomas, but he still told him to stop doubting. Nowhere is doubting God's revealed truth *approved* as a state of mind. The biblical guidance as to how to deal with doubt is therefore simple: stop it! We are not to doubt our Lord Jesus. We have given our lives to him and we are to grow in trust in him, repenting of all wrong attitudes including doubt (which we have distinguished from honestly asking sincere questions and looking to the Lord to answer them).

Many of the answers we need are in the Bible, and as we continue to study it, seeking the in-filling and guidance of the Holy Spirit, then we can be confident that any doubting thoughts will disappear and trust will grow.

Good Bible-believing Christian friends and pastors may be able to help us along the way.

John **20**:24–29; Matthew **14**:29–31; 1 Peter **5**:8–11

37
GROWING COLD

Background

In our love for the Lord (as in any love-relationship), devotion can wane. We find ourselves 'slipping' – losing our spiritual glow (cf. 1 Thessalonians 5:19). If we are not careful, the slipping becomes backsliding; and this is a very dangerous spiritual state as it can eventually lead to willful apostasy – a form of spiritual 'divorce'. We have to be on our guard so that we do not develop a cold heart towards the Lord Jesus.

What are some of the things to watch out for so that we do not grow cold spiritually?

Unbelief Mark 6:5–6; Hebrews 3:12; Jude 1:5

Bitterness Hebrews 12:15

Unforgiveness Matthew 5:23–24, 6:12; Romans 12:19–20

Cherishing sin Psalm 66:18

Sinful relationships 2 Corinthians 6:14–15 (but see 1 Corinthians 5:9–10!)

Satan's activity Matthew 4:3; Luke 8:12

Pride and snobbery Luke 18:9–14; John 5:44; Romans 10:3; 1 Corinthians 8:2–3; 1 John 1:8–10; Revelation 3:17–18

Argumentativeness Matthew 16:8; Romans 14:1; 2 Timothy 2:14, 16, 23

Worry Matthew 6:31, 34; Philippians 4:6–7

Debts Romans 13:8

Bad conscience Acts **24**:16; 1Timothy **1**:19, **3**:9; Titus **1**:15

Impurity Mark **7**:20–23; 1 Corinthians **9**:24–27; **10**:6,13

Gossiping (which can include 'confessing' other people's faults, real or imagined) Leviticus **19**:16; Psalm **101**:5; Romans **1**:29–30; James **3**:2–10

Neglect of prayer Matthew **26**:41; Luke **21**:36

Other priorities Matthew **6**:33, **13**:22

Ungodly influences Matthew **24**:12

What is the remedy?

All sin clouds our relationship with the Lord, but it is clinging to it which is the ongoing problem. The Lord knows our frailty and is quick to forgive when we repent (Psalm **103**:8–14) – which includes turning from whatever sin we may have been committing. However, when we are slow to confess our sin we are treating our relationship with the Lord as unimportant, and that offends him. We become estranged. If tempted to backslide, we need to heed the warning in Hebrews **10**:26–31.

The remedy lies in our being quick to come to the Lord Jesus for forgiveness and restoration when we become aware of sin and of coldness towards him. Be alert! Falling into sin is one thing: being willing to live with it in our lives is quite another. Acceptance of sin leads to coldness.

It is vital that our relationship with the Lord is cultivated as our absolute priority and, as we saw in Unit 25 (*Love*), our love for him is not just an emotional kind of 'love' relationship, there is a connection with *obedience* to him. "If you love [agape] me, keep my commandments" (John **14**:15); and, *"If you keep my commandments, you will abide in my* [agape] *love, just as I have kept my Father's commandments and abide in his love"* (John **15**:10).

1 Corinthians **9**:26–27; Philippians **3**:14; 1 Timothy **6**:12, **2**:8; Hebrews **12**:1

38

THE FLESH

When the Bible uses the word 'flesh' metaphorically it is referring to the nature we were born with. We inherited this nature from fallen Adam and so we have a natural leaning towards sin. Even when we are *born again*, (we must be if we are to see the kingdom of God; see John **3**:3) the 'sinful nature' (NIV) or 'old man/self' is not removed and it comes into conflict with our new spiritual nature. If we do not hold it in check and triumph over it, we will become 'carnal' or 'worldly'. Scripture calls this 'walking according to the flesh'.

The flesh is like a burden on a person's back

– rather as Romans tortured murderers by tying on their backs the corpse of their victim. (This amounted to a slow death sentence, a 'living death', and may be referred to in Romans **7**:24.)

Genesis **1**:27; **5**:3; Psalm **51**:5; John **3**:6; Romans **7**:14–24; Ephesians **2**:3

How is 'the flesh' or sinful nature overcome?

First of all we need to be born again and thus to receive a new nature. Then we begin to live 'in Christ' and we can be baptised in Holy Spirit and can go on being filled with Holy Spirit. It is the Holy Spirit who gives us the power to be holy and throw off slavery to the flesh and sin. However, we shall only be enabled to be victorious over the flesh if we are fully devoted to the Lord and choose to live in step with the Spirit, obeying the law of Christ, going on believing in him. Abiding in Christ, with the help of the Spirit, we can win battles over the old sinful self.

Genesis 4:7; Psalm 55:22; John 1:12–13; 6:63; Romans 6:4, 6–8; 7:4–6; 8:5–6; 13:14; Ephesians 5:8–15

The regenerate person belongs to Christ

Christ gives new life to those who repent and believe in him, and the new believer should want to please the Lord by walking closely with him and starving the old nature (the flesh). Our old self was crucified with Christ (see Romans 6:5).

If we are to experience continual victory over the flesh we cannot do this just by our own efforts but by constantly and consciously relying on the Holy Spirit to strengthen us. We are to live 'according to the Spirit'. We need to remember that in baptism we were baptised into the death of Jesus Christ who was raised from the dead, so that we may live a new life in Christ.

Romans 6:6; 7:21–25; 8:1–4, 8–10; 1 Corinthians 3:1–4; 2 Corinthians 7:1; 10:3–4; Galatians 2:20; 3:3; 5:1,16–17; Ephesians 5:24–25; 6:11–12

– and must no longer walk according to the flesh

If believers become 'carnal' ('fleshly') in their lives, they will bear such 'fruits' as selfishness, jealousy, rivalry, divisions, and they are being defeated by sin. They are not glorifying their Saviour and may fall away.

1 Corinthians 1:11–12; 3:1–4; 2 Corinthians 12:20–21; Philippians 1:15–17; 1 John 2:16; Revelation 3:15, 19

39
HYPOCRISY

Background

'Hypocrisy' comes from the Greek word for 'play-acting'. The actor is not really the person he or she is playing. In a stage drama we might think highly of good acting, but in reality such pretence is not virtuous – making out that we are what we are not. This is what 'hypocrisy' means in English: being false. As such it is seen in the Bible as a sin, especially when it takes the form of religious pretence. Religion can be put on like an actor's mask or costume in a vain attempt to fool God, others, or even ourselves.

Whilst hypocrisy is deplored in the Old Testament, particularly when it emerges in the form of insincere worship, it comes in for especially strong criticism in the New Testament. Jesus continually exposed this sin. It goes hand-in-hand with adopting a form of religion without it being inwardly true. The hypocrite can even fool himself and be blind to his own spiritual pretence, so that he is in danger of sealing his own eternal ruin. Lacking the real power of the Spirit in their lives, some 'Christians' act out a part – perhaps through outward forms of religion such as ritual or through pious talk and empty claims. One of the gravest sins in God's sight, it is a sin of 'attitude' (of a false heart) more than of 'action' (false deeds). Hypocritical acts spring from a hypocritical heart. In our Lord's teaching it is especially singled out as deserving hell.

Matthew **6**:2, 5, 16; **7**:5, 15; **15**:7–9; **23**:5–33; **24**:51; Mark **12**:15; Luke **12**:1–2; **13**:15; Acts **5**:1–11; Romans **12**:9; James **3**:17; 1 Peter **1**:22; 1 Peter **2**:1

Hypocrisy and counterfeit Christianity will be particularly widespread in the last days before Christ's Return

1 Timothy **4**:1–3; 2 Timothy **3**:1, 5

Counterfeit Christians

Some may masquerade as:

False Christs	Matthew **24**:24
False apostles	2 Corinthians **11**:13
False prophets	Matthew **24**:11, 24; 2 Peter **2**:1; 1 John **4**:1
False evangelists a false gospel)	Galatians **1**:6-9 (those who preach
False pastors	Acts **20**:29-30
False teachers	2 Peter **2**:1
False brothers	2 Corinthians **11**:26; Galatians **2**:4

Whilst we are to be aware of the possibility of hypocrisy in all its religious forms, we should be especially alert for hypocrisy in ourselves.

40
LEAVEN (OR YEAST)

Background

Leaven (or yeast) is a substance added to dough to make it ferment and rise. Only a small quantity is required for this purpose. The use of leaven in the making of bread was known to the ancient Hebrews. Leavening took time and was of no use when there was a need to make a hurried meal. From the earliest times the Hebrews attached spiritual meaning to leaven and associated the leavening process with creeping corruption. Even the smallest quantity was forbidden in Jewish houses at the time of the Feast of Unleavened Bread, which followed on from the Feast of Passover and which represented the requirement of the redeemed to live holy lives in communion with God and the covenant community.

Nor could it be in any offering which pointed forward to the propitiatory sacrifice of Christ, the sinless Lamb of God. In the Old Testament the presence of 'leaven' often suggests evil.

Genesis **19**:1–3 (cf. **18**:6); Exodus **12**:8, 11; **12**:14–15, 34–39; **13**:3, 6–7; **23**:18; Leviticus **2**:11; **6**:17; **10**:12; **23**:6–8; Numbers **6**:13–20; Deuteronomy **16**:3–8; Judges **6**:19–22; Hosea **7**:4

The New Testament

In the New Testament, leaven is often associated symbolically with false teaching and hypocrisy – an outward faith that has no corresponding inner reality. Jesus warns against the leaven of the Pharisees and others. Just as leaven works in a hidden way to permeate the dough and increase its mass, so corruption can be an unheeded process which gradually spreads and bloats.

However, we also note that Jesus uses the picture of leaven to help explain the meaning of the kingdom (see Matthew **13**:33; Luke **13**:20–21). This parable of the kingdom is in the context of pictures of growth. The kingdom will spread as yeast makes the dough grow.

The New Testament made it clear that false teaching and influences would infiltrate and adulterate the organised 'church'. Institutionally, it would become bloated in time by many nominal adherents (some 'members' not truly belonging to Christ) and by much external 'religion'.

Christians should be wary of the spread of corrupting elements and seek to live holy lives as the true redeemed of the Lord.

Matthew **16**:6, 11–12; Mark **8**:15; Luke **12**:1–3; **13**:20–21; 1 Corinthians **5**:6–13; Galatians **5**:7–9 (cf. also 2 Corinthians **7**:1; 2 Timothy **4**:3–4; 2 Peter **2**:1–2)

41

GIVING

Background

Christian giving from our resources (whether they are time, energies, possessions or money) is our grateful response to God's overwhelming generosity towards us, especially in his inexpressible gift of his Son to be our Saviour. Giving needs to be prompted by a regenerated heart of love and devotion to the Lord.

The Old Testament period

On one occasion Abraham gave Melchizedek one-tenth of some goods he had acquired (see Genesis **14**:20). The detail in the description of this action in Hebrews **7**:4–9 indicates that it does not amount to a precedent for tithing by people under the *Messianic covenant*.

Under the *Mosaic covenant*, one-tenth (a 'tithe') of agricultural produce 'belonged to the Lord' (see Leviticus **27**:30–32). See also Numbers **18**:21, 24; and see below for the use to which this portion was put.

Tithes were not the only goods given to the Lord (see Deuteronomy **12**:4–7). In Deuteronomy **14**:22–29 we see that the people ate tithe produce along with the firstborn livestock in the presence of God. The needs of the levitical priesthood were not to be neglected. There were freewill offerings as well as prescribed sacrifices. However, in Malachi **3**:8–10 we learn that neglect of the legal duty of the Jewish people under the *Mosaic covenant* in this matter was serious. In the expression 'the floodgates of heaven' we have a description of the rain which, of course, was needed for the growth of the produce and feeding of the flocks and herds.

See also Nehemiah **10**:37-39; **13**:10–12; Proverbs **3**:9.

We do not find a duty to tithe being laid upon the poor who may have been landless labourers. This should caution against direct application of the tithing law of the *Mosaic covenant* to Christians today who are living in a 'better covenant' (see Hebrews **7**:22) 'founded on better promises' (Hebrews **8**:6). Note especially that there was provision for the poor to help themselves from the corners of fields and food that was not picked up during harvesting. They would not have tithed from the gleanings! Tithes were from farmers and growers who grew crops and kept livestock. See Deuteronomy **24**:19–21. (See Note 1.) In the old covenant context, tithing was God's provision for the poor – including Levites (with no inheritance of their own) whose work was to offer sacrifices. (See Deuteronomy **14**:28-29; **16**:11, 14; **26**:11–13). In that setting it would have been a merciful, compassionate provision.

The New Testament

Christ exposed the Pharisaical abuse of tithing (see Matthew **23**:23–25). This formed part of a series of 'woes' Jesus uttered over people who were interested in externals but whose heart attitudes were wrong.

There is no legal obligation on Christians to give one-tenth of produce (or money income) to a Christian fellowship, church or leadership. As we note below, our responsibility under the *Messianic covenant* is considerably greater in character. In Unit 27 (*The Priesthood*) we learn that each believer is to offer himself or herself as a 'spiritual sacrifice' (Romans **12**:1). We belong to Jesus Christ. We live 'in him'. Everything believers are – and all that they have – belongs to him. The New Testament makes it clear that the levitical priesthood (for whose sustenance the legal tithes of the Law of Moses were prescribed) does not exist amongst believers in Jesus Christ. There is now a priesthood of all believers, and our great High Priest is Jesus Christ himself. Christian ministers are not like the sacrificing priests of the Old Testament. We recall that Paul the Apostle supported himself by tentmaking.

Some Christians tithe to their churches today because some church leaders teach it as though it were a legal requirement. However, there are serious dangers in teaching as a regulation what is not shown in the New Testament to be the 'Law of Christ'. Churches sometimes (wrongly) place an excessive burden on poor people. This is not to say that the poor should never give (we remember Jesus' approval of the donation by a poor woman in the account of the 'widow's mite') but to caution against legalistic burdens being placed by some Christians on others. We can find much guidance throughout the Bible concerning the special care due to the poor and needy, including many widows and orphans.

We are shown a new way in the New Testament. At Pentecost the new motive was revealed as people began to give spontaneously as they were prompted by God's grace and by love both for Christ and for their fellow believers.

The early church began to have 'all things' in common. There was real sharing and believers were providing for each other as brothers and sisters had need (see Acts **2**:44). Organised provision was then made for widows, who would have found life especially hard (see Acts **6**:1). But believers still had responsibilities towards other members of their own households (see 1 Timothy **5**:8).

Some even gave all they had, selling property and giving the proceeds. However, the sin of lying to the Holy Spirit was severely punished by God in the case of Ananias and Sapphira, who attempted deception about the scale of their giving (Acts **5**:1–11).

Matthew **6**:1–4; **10**:42; **19**:20–22; Luke **11**:42, **18**:12; Acts **2**:44–46, **4**:32, 34–37; 1 Corinthians **13**:3

True giving flows from the activity of the Holy Spirit. The will to give generously (especially to meet the needs of our brothers and sisters in Christ) arises from God's gracious work in the heart. It stems from true love for the Lord and from compassion for people in need (of whatever kind), especially our fellow believers. Where the Holy Spirit is powerfully at work there is invariably generous giving. We surrender all that we have to God in the realisation that it actually comes from him and belongs to him. We see ourselves as his stewards, privileged to be his agents of blessing. So we should seek his guidance as to how much we should give and to whom. For some this will actually be much more than ten percent of their income; for some who are destitute and unable to work, there needs to be the humility to receive gifts from others thankfully, without 'pride' getting in the way. We are all to give thanks to God, for ultimately it is he who meets all our needs, and we are all to be generous with whatever resources are at our disposal.

Dimensions of Christian Giving

Basis
Honest work	Ephesians **4**:28
Divine example	2 Corinthians **8**:9, **9**:15
Divine expectation	Matthew **6**:2; 1 Corinthians **16**:2
Divine enabling	2 Corinthians **9**:8-9
Divine quickening –	
To works of grace	2 Corinthians **8**:6–7,19
To acts of love	1 Corinthians **13**:3
Divine generosity	1 Corinthians **4**:7

Extent
Every believer	1 Corinthians **16**:2
Proportionate	1 Corinthians **16**:2; 2 Corinthians
8:3, 12–15	

Motivation
God's glory	2 Corinthians **8**:19; **9**:11–13

GIVING

Manner

Generously	2 Corinthians **9**:6
Voluntarily	2 Corinthians **8**:3,8; **9**:7
Cheerfully	2 Corinthians **9**:7
Discreetly	Matthew **6**:1–4
Sincerely	Acts **5**:1–11; Romans **12**:8
Habitually	1 Corinthians **16**:2

Beneficiaries

Those who ask — Matthew **5**:42

Those in need
(especially believers) — 2 Corinthians **9**:1; Galatians **6**:10; James **2**:15–17; 1 John **3**:17

Those in ministry — 1 Corinthians **9**:14; Galatians **6**:6; Philippians **4**:10,14–18; 1 Timothy **5**:17–18

Rewards

Divine blessing	2 Corinthians **9**:10–11
Heavenly treasure	Matthew **19**:21
Present happiness	Acts **20**:35; 2 Corinthians **9**:11–12

Note

[1] For further study, with many useful additional biblical references, the following PDF ebook is currently available for free download: Russell E. Kelly Ph.D., *Should the Church Teach Tithing?* ISBN: 978-0-595-15978-9

42

INSPIRATION OF SCRIPTURE

Background

The Bible is totally trustworthy because God himself is its ultimate Author and Authority. That is why we call it 'the Word of God'. God has revealed that he exists as Creator of the universe (and men can work this out from the very fact that the universe exists and requires a cause outside itself), but mankind is finite and fallen and so is unable to have a perfect and personal knowledge of God without his further revelation of himself in his written Word and supremely in his living Word, the incarnate Son, Jesus Christ. God has used human writers as his means of revelation in Scripture. He has used those he raised up and stirred to write the Scriptures. God the Holy Spirit overshadowed, directed and 'carried along' (2 Peter **1**:21) the human writers of Scripture (we might think of the wind in the sails of a ship) so that what they originally wrote was preserved from all error. This divine activity in and through the human writers is what we call 'inspiration' – though 2 Timothy **3**:16 is more accurately translated: *All Scripture is breathed out by God*. Thus, the sixty-six books of the Bible (not including the Apocrypha) are authored and authenticated by God and are to be the supreme authority in our thinking, teaching and living. All biblical study and scholarship should reverently submit to that authority as it seeks to understand and expound the teaching of Scripture.

The Bible claims clearly to be God's Word to man
Again and again we read, "Thus says the Lord", or, "The word of the Lord that came to . . ." this prophet or that.

Exodus **4**:15; **24**:4, 7; **32**:16; Deuteronomy **31**:24–26; Psalm **68**:11; Isaiah **1**:2; **28**:14,16; Jeremiah **5**:14 (and many others); Ezekiel **2**:7, **3**:3; Zechariah **7**:7; 1 Thessalonians **2**:13; 2 Timothy **3**:16; 2 Peter **1**:16–21

This revealing of God's Word through human agents (or prophets) continues right up to the end of the Bible – to God's final revelation, now given by God's incarnate Word (John 1:1) Jesus, who is God's Son. He addresses his Church.

Revelation **1**:1, 19; **2**:1, 8, 12, 18; **3**:1, 7, 14; **21**: 5; **22**:16

The human authors testify to certain occasions when a direct command from God was given to them to write, and Paul insists that his message, both spoken and written, came direct from God.

Moses – Exodus **17**:14

Isaiah – Isaiah **8**:1; **30**:8

Jeremiah – Jeremiah **30**:1–2; **36**:1–32

Habakkuk – Habakkuk **2**:2

John – Revelation **1**:1–3, 19; **21**:5

Paul – Romans **16**:25-26; 1 Corinthians **2**:7–15; **11**:23; **14**:37; Galatians **1**:11–12; Ephesians 3:3–4; 1 Thessalonians **2**:13; **4**:15; 1 Timothy **4**:1

Christ's words witness to the divine authorship of the Old Testament. He also claimed the full authority of his Father for all his own utterances.

Matthew **4**:4; **5**:18; **19**:4, 7; **22**:31–32, 43–45; **26**:54; Luke **4**:21; **24**:25, 27, 44–45; John **5**:46–47; **8**:47; **12**:48; **16**:12–13; **17**:8; **10**:35

The Bible speaks as having divine authority, and people may be convicted of sin as they read it. The Bible is capable of revealing the meaning intended by God in every age and in every circumstance in which a person may find himself, provided that person is willing to be taught by the Holy Spirit. God has commanded the Bible to be read and taught.

Joshua **1**:8; 2 Kings **23**:2, 24; Psalm **1**:1–2; **119**:105; Acts

17:11; Romans **15**:4; 1 Corinthians **2**:14–15; Ephesians **6**:17; Colossians **4**:16; 1 Thessalonians **5**:27; 1 Timothy **4**:13; 2 Timothy **3**:15–16; **4**:2; James **1**:21–22

There is a solemn warning to those who add to, or take away from, the words of the Bible.

Deuteronomy **4**:2; Mark **7**:13; Revelation **22**:18–19

Notes

"The implications of inspiration were not questioned until relatively recently. Until the second half of the nineteenth century on no subject had the Church been more united" (T C Hammond & David F Wright, *In Understanding Be Men*).

Some appeal to the 'three-legged stool' of Scripture + Reason + Tradition, but Scripture is <u>paramount</u> over human reason and church tradition because it is '*God*-breathed' [Gk. *Theopneustos*; 2 Timothy **3**:16].

The following points must be remembered when studying the question of the inspiration of the Bible:

a) It is the original writings that were inspired. Translation and transmission are not equally free from error.

b) The record itself is inspired, even though it sometimes includes mention of things which oppose him. For instance, there were some who said of Jesus: *"He has a demon, and is insane"* (John **10**:20). This was not the truth, but the record of it is inspired.

c) There are different kinds of composition in Scripture, such as history, poetry and parable, each of which must be understood in the light of the plain meaning in context.

d) 2 Peter **1**:20 makes an important point when it says that, '. . . no prophecy of Scripture came about by the prophet's own interpretation of things.' We are neither to be subjective in our interpretation (ignoring the clear meaning), nor must we take one verse in isolation from the rest of the passage – and indeed the particular book and the Bible as a whole. The Psalmist tells us:

> *All your words are true;*
> *all your righteous laws are eternal*
> (Psalm **119**:160, *NIV*)

43
SATAN

Background

Satan (= 'adversary'), or the Devil (= 'slanderer'), is given numerous different titles and names in the Bible, e.g. Matthew **10**:25; **12**:24; 2 Corinthians **4**:4 ; **6**:15; John **12**:31; **14**:30; Ephesians **2**:2; Revelation **9**:11; **12**:9; **20**:2 with Genesis **3**. Clearly, the Bible is speaking about a person and not just a principle of evil. Who and what is that person?

Identity and Origin

The Bible reveals to us his identity, but it does so through hints and gives him no more attention than is necessary. For instance, the Greek of John **8**:44 says that he did not 'stand in the truth', which implies that he fell into sin; and Luke **10**:18 speaks of his downfall from heaven. He seems to have been a high-ranking angelic being who rebelled against God's rule and was thrown out of heaven along with his angel-supporters (who became the demons). When God created man and gave him intimate fellowship, Satan seems to have resented this and – taking the form of a beautiful serpent – seduced Eve with Adam into sin. He is constantly trying to corrupt God's world spitefully.

Isaiah **14**:12–15 (where Satan is seen as the power behind the King of Babylon); Ezekiel **28**:12-19 (where he is seen as the power behind the King of Tyre); Luke **10**:18; Revelation **12**:4, 7–9; Genesis **3**:1–15

Character

Satan is revealed as:
- arrogant (his rebellion against God; 1 Timothy **3**:6)
- wicked (Ephesians **6**:12; 1 John **2**:13; **3**:8)

- wily (Genesis **3**:1; 2 Corinthians **11**:3; Ephesians **6**:11)
- deceitful (John **8**:44; 2 Corinthians **11**:14; Revelation **12**:9)
- fiercely destructive (like a wolf – John **10**:12, a lion – 1 Peter **5**:8, and a dragon – Revelation **12**:9; **20**:2).

Activity

Impenitent in his sin, Satan is opposed to God and God's kingdom. Though his power is vastly less than that of the Lord who created him in the first place, he and his demons can still cause plenty of trouble as God allows them to act until the divine purpose has been fulfilled. We note that Satan was instrumental in events which led to—
- the downfall of a large minority of angels (Revelation **12**:4, 7-9)
- the Fall of mankind (Genesis **3**)
- the curse on the cosmos (Genesis **3**:17–19; but see also Romans **8**:19–22).

Satan—
- rules over the demons (Matthew **12**:24)
- opposed Jesus, the Incarnate Lord (Matthew **4**:1–11; John **13**:27)
- opposes the gospel and Christ's Church
  – by holding unbelievers captive (1 Timothy **3**:7; 2 Timothy **2**:26; Hebrews **2**:14–17; 1 John **5**:19)
  – by blinding unbelievers (Matthew **13**:19; John **8**:43–45; 2 Corinthians **4**:4)
  – by counterfeiting the truth (thereby causing cults, heresies, schisms and factions)
  (Matthew **7**:15, **24**:11, 24; Acts **20**:29–30; 2 Corinthians **11**:13, 14; Galatians **1**:6–9; 2 Thessalonians **2**:3–4, 9–12; Matthew **24**:24; 2 Peter **2**:1)
- hinders Christian workers (1 Thessalonians **2**:18)
- seduces Christians into sin (1 Thessalonians **3**:5)
- demoralises Christians with his accusations (Revelation **12**:10).

Power of the enemy over believers is *strictly limited*.

What are we to do . . . ?

Satan did not reckon with God's grace. The Lord had a plan of salvation to redeem sinners who could enjoy victorious living by their—

- *relying* on Christ's atoning work on the cross of Calvary on their behalf (Revelation **12**:11)
- in the power of God, *resisting* Satan (Ephesians **4**:27; **6**:10–18; James **4**:7; 1 Peter **5**:9)
- *being* vigilant and prayerful (Matthew **26**:41).

Destiny

A defeated enemy, Satan is doomed and finally will be punished in hell.
Matthew **25**:41; Luke **10**:19; John **12**:31; **16**:11, 33; Romans **16**:20; Colossians **2**:15; Hebrews **2**:14; 2 Peter **2**:4; 1 John **3**:8, **4**:4; Jude **6**; Revelation **20**:2, 7, 10

44

THE SECOND COMING

Background

What do we mean by the 'Second Coming'? This means the visible return of Jesus, the Messiah, to this world – a still future event. Note that this study deals primarily with the future, so should be addressed with a sense of caution and humility. We need to recognise that although the fact of Jesus' return is certain, it is unwise to be too dogmatic about details.

How do we know that there will be a visible return of Jesus to this world?

The Old Testament clearly predicted the first coming of the Messiah, even giving details of his death (see especially Isaiah **52** and **53**). Yet the majority of the Hebrew nation was unprepared and blind to the things that were happening. The Bible is equally emphatic about Jesus' *visible return* – the second coming. Jesus himself referred to his second coming more than twenty times, and there are more than two hundred other such references in the New Testament. As Jesus fulfilled all the prophecies contained in the Old Testament concerning the coming of the Messiah, so will he fulfil prophecies relating to his second coming. See especially Acts **1**:11 and 1 Thessalonians **4**:14. *(See also the book entitled 'The Birth of Christ' also available free on the Glory to Glory website, and especially Appendix 3 relating to prophecies concerning the birth of the Messiah.)*

Psalm **22**:1, 7, 13–18; Matthew **24**:21–30; John **14**:3; Acts **1**:11; Romans **11**:25–26; 1 Corinthians **1**:7; Philippians **3**:20–21; 1 Thessalonians **1**:9–10; **2**:19; **3**:12–13; **4**:16, 18; Titus **2**:13; Hebrews **9**:28.

Before his return, certain things will have happened

A long time will pass after the first coming. Time is not a 'problem' for God, but it is a problem for humans! Matthew **24**:6–8, 48; **25**:5, 19.

Note that the scriptures emphasise the absolute necessity to be prepared for Christ's return at any moment – and of course he may take any of us at any time!

The Hebrew people will be preserved as a nation in dispersion. At the time of the end, they will return to the land that God promised to them. This has already begun to happen.

Deuteronomy **30**:3; Isaiah **11**:10–12; **60**:9; Jeremiah **30**:11, 18; **31**:10–13; Ezekiel **36**:24–36; **37**:1–11; Luke **21**:24 (many consider that the time of the Gentiles has now ended); Romans **11**:25 (there will be an increasing turning among Jewish people to their Lord – *Yeshua* [the Hebrew name for Jesus]).

The gospel of Jesus must have been proclaimed across the entire world. This again has now virtually happened. Although not completely fulfilled, this emphasises the urgency of missionary work. Matthew **24**:14; Mark **16**:15.

Many false religions will arise – some in the name of Jesus. Religions will be marked out by their refusal to acknowledge the deity of Jesus, the truth of his propitiatory death on the cross, or the truth of his resurrection from death. Some sects and religions will align themselves with what may be called normative Christianity, although it must be noted that the very term 'Christian' is now inadequate to truly describe the disciples of Jesus. There will be a new emphasis on aligning the religions and preaching that ultimately they are all one, under God. This is a heresy, but will be encountered more and more in the future. Matthew **24**:5, 11, 24; Luke **17**:23; 2 Thessalonians **2**:3; 2 Peter **2**:1–3.

The times of the Gentiles must have run its course. Gentile domination of Jerusalem and the ancient lands of Israel will end – Luke **21**:24. Jesus described the approach of his return as being like *birth pangs*. The pangs arise so we know that something is about to happen. Jesus' explanation of the future is contained in Matthew chapter **24**, which students may want to pause to read in its entirety.

At the time of his return certain things will be happening

Unprecedented calamities – earthquakes and associated societal dislocations, political crises, godlessness, persecution of the true followers of Jesus, whether Jewish or Gentile. These will be unprecedented in the sense that their intensity will increase, there will be more of them and they will happen together. Daniel **12**:9–10; Joel **2**:31; Zephaniah **1**:14–18; Matthew **24**:9–10, 21; Luke **21**:11, 25; 2 Timothy **3**:1–5.

Organised Christianity will be absorbed in the world. There will be global apostasy – a turning away from Christ to other things. Christian 'religion' will become in different ways cold, formal, asleep, or aligned to other religions. Sadly, the so-called church will be as unprepared for the *Second Coming* as the Hebrew religious leaders were for the *first* coming. In both cases the religious leaders should have been alert and aware. In the past they were not. In the future (present?) they apparently are not. Matthew **24**:3–4, 9, 12, 24, 44; **25**:1–13; Mark **13**:36; Luke **17**:26–27, 30; **18**:8; **21**:34–35; 1 Thessalonians **5**:1–6; 2 Peter **3**:3–4; Revelation **3**:15–18.

There will be a worldwide fear for the future. Luke **21**:25–26.

Some believers will be expecting his return. There will be a hidden remnant that will be ready, waiting and scattered across the world, from all races. Daniel **12**:9–10; Matthew **25**:1–3, 8; Luke **21**:35–36.

There will have been a return to Israel of Jewish people on a large scale. Isaiah **11**:11–12; Ezekiel **37**:11, 14, 21–22.

A global dictator and religious leader will appear. It has been suggested that he may arise in Europe, but we should not be dogmatic about this. He will gain worldwide power. He will be religiously followed – and feared. After being victorious he will have designs upon Israel. This leader may be aligned with, or may be identical to, the apostate leader of a reunited 'Christendom' – the Antichrist. This person may be the ultimate architect of harmonised religion, or out of the religions he may form a new, final, false religion. Daniel **7**:8 (the 'little horn' is the Antichrist); **11**:36–45; **12**:1; Matthew **24**:14–16; 2 Thessalonians **2**:3–12; Revelation **13**:3–18; **19**:17–20.

Again we emphasise in relation to the above that it is unwise to be too dogmatic about the details, but the general outline is plain to see – there will be a global politico-religious leader/ship that is in opposition to Christ – and ultimately this will be destroyed by Christ.

The world will be in the throes of a final great war – a war ultimately against God, involving the Jewish people in some way, and centered on the land of Israel. This is called 'Armageddon'. Israel will be seen as defenceless. Many Jewish people will turn to Jesus (Yeshua) as their Messiah, because of the great distress at that time. But the Lord will have the final word in this. The enemy will not prevail. Ezekiel **38**:8–12, 15, 21–22; Joel **3**:1–2, 9–11, 14; Zechariah **12**:1–10; **14**:1–9; Romans **11**:26–27; Revelation **16**:14, 16.

Note

Some argue that elements of these prophecies have already passed. Overall this seems not to be the case. But *some* prophecies certainly did have both a short-term outworking, and a second longer-term outworking. Some of the prophecies referred to in this study may be in short- and long-term categories. The short-term outworking would have been in biblical times, but the future outworking is still awaited.

The second coming of the Lord

There are a number of interpretations of what the Bible says. Again we would caution against being overly or destructively/ divisively dogmatic about this. What we can say is that the return will be **visible, dramatic and definitive**. It will be a surprise to the world at large – and to many in the church, it seems. To most it will come *like a thief in the night* (1 Thessalonians **5**:2–4). No one expects a thief, or they would be ready for him! The second coming will glorify the Lord. His true Church, his bride – his 'called-out' from all nations, races and tongues – will now at last be triumphant. The precise details are somewhat mysterious but most Bible-believing Christians would generally recognise the following:

Jesus' disciples will be called in some visible, separate way. Luke **17**:24, 34–36; 1 Corinthians **15**:51–53; 1 Thessalonians **4**:13–17.

The Lord's physical return is clear. Zechariah **14**:4–5; 1 Thessalonians **3**:13.

The second coming. Matthew **24**:27–31, 39; **25**:6, 13, 23–31; Luke **12**:39–40; **21**:27–28, 34–35; Acts **1**:7, 10–11; Colossians **3**:4; 1 Peter **5**:4; 1 John **2**:28.

A period of Christ's rule on earth. Isaiah **11**:6–9; Jeremiah **23**:5–6; Zechariah **14**:9; Revelation **20**:1–4.

The End

The destruction of evil, the judgment, and the end of the present earth. Hebrews **1**:10–12; 2 Peter **3**:10–13; Revelation **20**:7–14.

A new heaven and a new earth. 1 Corinthians **15**:24–28; Revelation **21**:1, 4.

Final prayer – Revelation **22**:20 *Amen. Come, Lord Jesus.*

Further Reading Pawson, D, *Living in Hope* (Terra Nova, 2008) provides a useful study of Matthew 23–24.

45

WINE – A BIBLICAL PERSPECTIVE

Background

In both the Old and New Testaments, the proper (moderate) use of wine – the fermented product of grapes – is depicted as a normal feature of the life of God's people, but excessive use (drunkenness) is shown to be sinful.

Historically, abuse of many kinds of alcoholic beverages became a serious social problem during many periods, especially during and following the Industrial Revolution in large British cities, and in many early pioneer communities that spread out across America. Some evangelists, aware of the dire individual and communal effects stemming from drunkenness (including disease, child neglect, violence, other anti-social behaviour and family break-up) made abstinence from *all* forms of alcohol a feature of their preaching and teaching, accompanying the call to repentance and commitment to Christ. Methodism, the Salvation Army and (in North America especially) much independent revivalist preaching, have been associated with this linkage of themes. Undoubtedly, appeals to abstinence or temperance helped many who were misusing strong alcoholic drinks, especially distilled spirits. Consequently, countless folk who responded to such appeals to personal faith in Christ along with a call to repent of drunkenness would have experienced a beneficial transformation in their personal lifestyles and family lives at the same time as their hearts were being changed by hearing and responding to the gospel.[1]

Social, personal and family benefits accrued from the radical change in many individuals who had been prone to drunkenness – a move from serious abuse of alcohol to complete abstinence from all alcoholic drinks. This led in some quarters to a dogmatism on the subject of abstinence which, as we will see, cannot be supported by the scriptural evidence, and indeed ignores the perfect example of our Lord Jesus Christ himself, concerning the proper, moderate taking of wine with a meal, so well attested in Jewish life (past and present). Today, in European and Mediterranean societies the cultural custom of moderate drinking of a glass or two of wine with a meal continues. In many other societies, where the culture has never been that of moderate wine consumption, distilled spirits and beer can very often pose a threat to health and social well-being. There is a huge distinction between proper use and abuse, and the Bible depicts both very clearly in many passages.

Genesis **9**:20–21; **27**:37; Psalm **80**:8–19; Jeremiah **2**:21–25 (although a choice vine, Israel rebels); Proverbs **23**:21, 29–35; Isaiah **5**:11–12; Habakkuk **2**:15 (the allegorical reference here is to the shame that follows drunkenness)

A gift from God

God's gifts in creation can be (and indeed often are) misused. Wine is no exception to this general principle, but let us start with the right use first, before we return to the matter of sinful misuse.

Wine (along with olive oil, grain crops and dairy produce) was rightly seen by God's ancient chosen people as a blessing in creation. (See, for example, Deuteronomy **7**:13; **11**:14.) Vineyards are mentioned many times in Scripture, as are winepresses, because wine consumption was a perfectly normal feature of Hebrew life. In Isaiah chapter 5 the construction of a vineyard provides a vivid analogy. In the New Testament there is no embarrassment when artefacts used in the storage and transportation of wine ('wineskins') are mentioned to illustrate an important point (Luke **5**:37). At his first great miracle at Cana, Jesus turned water into good wine, which was enjoyable for the community as they shared a celebration at the wedding feast (John **2**:1-11).Not only was wine the customary drink in the everyday life of the Hebrew people, it was also used to commemorate the mighty acts of God. In the present day as in ancient times, wine is used in the Jewish Passover celebrations. This is part of normal Jewish family life, in which drunkenness would be extremely unlikely to feature.

At the Last Supper, wine was in the cup which Jesus gave to his disciples and they could look forward to the day when he will drink wine with them again, *"in my Father's kingdom"*. (See Matthew **26**:29.) Throughout the centuries since then, Christians have obeyed Jesus' command, using bread and wine at celebrations of the Lord's Supper to commemorate the Lord's saving death and resurrection until that Day when he shall come again in glory to judge the living and the dead.

The proper, moderate use of wine and the biblical prohibition of drunkenness may have been well-known to most Jews, but some of the new Gentile believers may have required more instruction in the matter. In matters of what we eat and drink, of course, we are not to legislate for other Christians, except to remind ourselves and others that what God prohibits (drunkenness, greed and sloth included, amongst other sinful lifestyles such as those marked by pride and unforgiveness) offend him and are very bad for us. God wants us to enable our brothers and sisters to have enough to enjoy his creation gifts appropriately, providing for the needy (e.g. 'widows and orphans') sharing his good gifts in his created order, especially with fellow-believers, and, particularly, for all of us to thank him for those gifts. Jesus gave thanks to the Father over bread and wine. We are to follow his example. In Jewish and Christian understanding, as is revealed in the Bible, God is very much interested in all the earthy practicalities of how we are living, and what our attitudes are – toward him and toward others.

Judges **9**:13; Esther **1**:10; Psalm **104**:15; Ecclesiastes **10**:19; Isaiah **55**:1–2; Zechariah **10**:7

The misuse of a gift

It is wise to eat appropriate amounts of a good, healthy range of fresh, natural foods, but if we eat excessively we commit the sin of gluttony and we also become more prone to many of the diseases which afflict the supposedly 'developed' world. By the same token, if we over-indulge in wine and other (perhaps much stronger) alcoholic drinks we may succumb to drunkenness (also condemned in Scripture) and again become more susceptible to another range of diseases and disorders. In matters of food and drink, wisdom and moderation are required, and excess should be avoided for both spiritual and health reasons. Again, we can reflect that the 'Maker's handbook' provides the best guidance to right behaviour in the areas of food and drink, as in every other area it addresses!

Isaiah **28**:1–8; Proverbs **20**:1; **21**:17; **23**:20; **23**:32–34

Legalistic prohibition

In Old Testament times, some minority sects practised total abstinence; other groups abstained from wine temporarily, when carrying out certain religious duties.

However, to teach that total abstinence from alcoholic beverages is a requirement of moral law or the 'law of Christ', or is somehow more 'Christian' than moderate consumption of wine with a meal, has no support whatsoever in Scripture, nor is it borne out by the teaching and practice of Jesus and the apostles. Such elevation of 'total abstinence' is in a very obvious sense legalistic, and it is an especially curious form of legalism in that it flies in the face not only of Jewish practice and observance, even the Passover celebration, but also, even more significantly, it runs counter to the perfect example of righteous living in the Son of God himself. Jesus never compromised the truth and he did not do a single unrighteous act. So, for Jesus, drinking wine moderately with a meal was not some sort of reluctant concession to, or participation in, a supposed 'vice'. That would be a manifestly absurd idea. On the contrary it was the right and proper exemplary enjoyment of social life with fellow-Jews of a gift in creation, revealed by the One who showed us all perfectly, firstly how we should live together with others in society; then in the community of faith (as in the eucharistic life of the church after Pentecost); and, finally, as an illustration of the future Messianic banquet in which believers will enjoy the best wine of all with our Lord when he personally governs his kingdom in a new heaven and earth. In none of this, the truly biblical picture, do we gain any notion that the drinking of the fermented fruit of the vine is evil (though people who misuse the gift by becoming drunk are sinning). It is, however, a point of view that is not unknown amongst those who trace their teaching tradition back to the evangelists and revivalists referred to in our 'background' paragraph above. To be fair to those who espouse such total abstinence, they are often speaking into a social context in which there is hazardous consumption of strong proof, distilled alcoholic drinks (such as whisky and other spirits) rather than the ordinary wine of the Ancient Near East. In conclusion, the Bible does not say or even suggest that total abstinence from alcoholic drinks is essential to salvation, so legalism must be avoided in this area. Nonetheless, where addiction (and, consequently, drunkenness) is or has been a particular personal problem, there are those who will be prudent to avoid the occasions of temptation. As always, the Bible student is encouraged to consider the biblical evidence.

Ephesians **5**:18; 1 Timothy **3**:8; **5**:23; Titus **2**:3

[1]Note

A line of argument used to be adopted in some quarters which suggested that biblical wine was not really wine as we know it today. However, whilst wine making techniques no doubt altered somewhat down the ages, it was obviously perfectly possible for people in the biblical era to have got drunk on wine or the risk of doing so would not have needed to be the subject of the warnings in both Testaments, spanning the relevant periods. That is clear from the biblical evidence.

46
PERSECUTION

Background

When we talk about the suffering church we refer to the persecuted church, in other words the church that suffers because it owns the name of Christ. It is true that sometimes believers suffer for other reasons — perhaps because of their own rebellion against God, perhaps because of their indifference to social or moral evil which leads in turn to spiritual weakness. In this study we consider suffering only in the context of persecution.

The people of God are no strangers to persecution. The entire Bible witnesses not only to God's goodness, justice and mercy, but also to the devil's opposition to God, which manifests itself in opposition to God's people in particular, and to humanity in general. Right back in the earliest parts of the Bible we see persecution of the righteous by the unrighteous. Righteousness stands in contrast — and opposition — to evil. Evil will not countenance righteousness and so opposes it.

In the Old Testament

The earliest persecution we encounter in the Bible was of Abel by his brother Cain, recorded in Genesis chapter 4. Abel's sacrifice was acceptable to God, whilst Cain's sacrifice was not. As men try to build their own righteousness before God, whether through politics, humanism, or false religions, these same men are angered by *the one sacrifice* that is acceptable to God, the sacrifice of Jesus Christ, God's Son. Cain murdered his brother on account of Abel's goodness compared to Cain's shabbiness. (And see Matthew **23**:35;

and 1 John **3**:12-13). The Old Testament is replete with stories of those who suffered for doing right. We think of Daniel, thrown to the lions, yet who was protected by God. We think of Moses, opposed along with his people, the Hebrews – opposed by Pharaoh, the ruler of Egypt. We think of the prophets, many of whom were martyred for delivering God's message without fear or favour to people and to leaders who did not want to listen. We think of David, persecuted by Saul because of God's obvious spiritual blessing of David.

We think of Nehemiah, opposed by Sanballat (and others) as he began to secure the holy city of Jerusalem. We think of Esther and the Jewish people persecuted by Haman, the King's official – reminding us of state opposition to those of faith down through history. Ultimately, those who persecute will fall.

Genesis **4**:1–16; Psalm **9**:13–16; Psalm **34**:17–22; Psalm **41** (many of the Psalms deal with the theme of suffering, and the context of persecution often lurks behind that suffering).

In the New Testament

The Lord Jesus made it very clear that persecution will often be experienced by those who put their trust in him.

Matthew **5**:3–12 (especially 11–12); **10**:17–42; Mark **13**:9; John **15**:18 to **16**:4

Jesus also made it clear that Christians should have a priority in caring for their brethren – and in this he seems to have had in mind, once again, suffering caused by persecution. Matthew **25**:31–46 is relevant in this context, and especially sobering are verses 44-5, where the neglect by the 'goats' appears to have referred to their brothers and sisters in Christ, even more so than any neglect of their neighbours in the wider world.

The early Christians' experience of persecution is described in many places in the New Testament. Jesus himself was persecuted – he was unjustly accused and convicted, suffered mockery and violence, and was executed by the appalling method of crucifixion (Mark **14**:43–**15**:37). The first church in Jerusalem was scattered by persecution (Acts **8**:1b–3) and two of its leaders were killed (Acts **7**:54–**8**:1; **12**:1–2).

In Paul's list of his sufferings for Christ, he includes imprisonment, flogging, beating and stoning (2 Corinthians **11**:23–25). Hebrews was written for Christians whose property had been confiscated (Hebrews **10**:34), and the readers of 1 Peter had to bear slander and insults (1 Peter **2**:12; **4**:3–4). The churches in Revelation had endured hardships including imprisonment and being killed. (Revelation **2**:9–10 and 13; cf. **6**:9–11).

Several New Testament writers look behind the human causes of persecution to draw out its significance for believers. The book of Revelation attributes some affliction to the devil (see Revelation **2**:10). God sets a limit to afflictions and he uses them to work out his plans. (See Acts **11**:19–21; 1 Thessalonians **3**:2–4; 1 Peter **5**:10).

Although persecution is inevitable for Christians, it is also a means of blessing for those who suffer it. The persecutions of Jesus' disciples is linked in the Gospels with the *labour pains of the age to come* (Matthew **24**:4–12). Those who are persecuted for the sake of righteousness are promised the kingdom of heaven (Matthew **5**:10). Paul affirms that those who suffer with Christ will also be glorified with him (Romans **8**:17). Nor is such blessing only for the future: suffering produces perseverance, character and hope in the present, so that believers can even rejoice in it. (See Romans **5**:3–4; James **1**:2–3).

Various responses to persecution are found in the New Testament, including flight, appealing to the authorities for protection, and faithful endurance. Different circumstances may call for different responses – even for the same person. So Paul escapes from Damascus when his life is endangered (Acts **9**:23–25, cf. 2 Corinthians **11**:32–33), and we are reminded of Jesus' instruction to disciples to flee when suffering persecution (Matthew **10**:23). But on another occasion Paul makes use of his Roman citizenship to appeal to the emperor, to avoid being handed over to his enemies (Acts **25**:11).

Persecution will end

The disciples are not left alone to face their enemies: Jesus will provide them with words and wisdom to defend themselves (Luke **21**:12–15). No one can snatch them out of his or his Father's hand (John **10**:28–29), and provided they stand firm to the end they will be saved (Matthew **24**:13). The first letter of Peter, taken in whole, is sometimes referred to as a manual for living under persecution. It is well worth reading in full with this understanding in mind.

God is not a loser. He will preserve for himself a Church and a holy nation, and those who have been martyred, men, women and children (as they have been all through history), will have a special place in the kingdom of heaven. Where do we learn about the end of the history of persecution? At the end of the Bible, of course! In Revelation chapter 6 we read of John the apostle's vision of the seals being opened. When the fifth seal is opened, he sees the souls of all those who had been slain because of the word of God and the testimony they had maintained. They ask God openly how long it will be before he judges and their blood is avenged. They are told to wait a little longer, until the last of the martyrs is gathered in to heaven. At **7**:13-17 (read this carefully) we discover the glorious climax. Finally, in **19**:6-9, we are shown that persecution is not the end: there is to be the wedding supper of the Lamb.

Our Lord Jesus will return for his bride, the Church. What an ending! Hallelujah indeed!

Note

This Study is closely linked to Unit 49, although much of the material is different, justifying two studies on related themes.

47

THE CHOSEN PEOPLE

Background

The understanding of 'the chosen people' is rooted in the Biblical teaching of God's election (calling) of Israel. Moses sings of Israel as 'the apple of God's eye' (Deuteronomy **32**:10) and Israel is declared time and time again in the Bible to have a special/chosen relationship with God (Exodus **4**:22; Psalm **105**:6; Jeremiah **31**:9 Hosea **11**:1).

The term 'Israel' was given to Jacob after he wrestled/strived with 'God' (see Genesis **32**:22–32). Later, Jacob's descendants became known as *bene Yisrael* (sons of Israel). However, the blessing of Israel predates Jacob and is initially linked to God's call of Abram, and his faithful covenantal promises to him (see Genesis **12**).

These promises are enlarged in the subsequent biblical covenants with Moses and David.

The new covenant follows (see Jeremiah **31**:31–34 and Hebrews **8**) and many divine promises and prophecies are fulfilled. Ultimately, all will be fulfilled when the Messiah returns.

Both the ancient people of God and believers in Jesus (Jews and Gentiles) received something from God: the Jews remember their people having been saved from slavery in Egypt (as well as receiving many great promises); believers in *Yeshua*, whether Jews or Gentiles, remember that they have been saved from the penalty of sin, are being saved from the power of sin, and will one day be saved from the presence of sin.

Election and covenants

Awareness of what the Bible teaches us about election and covenantal faithfulness is vital to our understanding of God's purposes and promises. Paul explores carefully this understanding in Romans **9–11** and affirms that the gifts and calling of God to his people are irrevocable (Romans **11**:29). He looks forward to the day when 'all Israel' will be saved. (See the chapter entitled 'Israel in Romans' in *Israel in the New Testament*[1] for a discussion of the important question as to what the expression 'all Israel' might actually mean in the context of Romans **11**:26.) Paul understands that the promises to Israel have been confirmed and not revoked in the ministry of Jesus Christ (see Romans **15**:8; 2 Corinthians **1**:20).

In New Testament teaching, Gentiles as well as Jews become part of the elect of God through faith in Jesus Christ, (see Ephesians **1**:4; **2**:11–22; 1 Peter **1**:1). It is also worth exploring that in the New Testament the term 'Israel' is used of *ethnic* Israel (Jacob's descendants) or the *faithful remnant* within Israel (see Romans **9**:6 and Romans **11**:2–5). The church is both the called out (ecclesia) community – (called out from the sin and unbelief of the world to witness and serve God's purposes) and the grafted in community (see the olive tree teaching in Romans **11**) to be built into a spiritual people and to serve as a holy priesthood (1 Peter **2**:4).

Sadly, ideas about election and those of a 'chosen people' can be misused. It is important to stress that God's election of Israel is primarily a gift for service and witness. Israel is to serve God as a distinctive (holy) community (see Deuteronomy **7**:6 and Joel **3**:16).This very point is made powerfully in Isaiah **49**:6.

In terms of the new (messianic) covenant, note that the language of election is (significantly) employed with hindsight, i.e. Christians look back on what God did for them in a way that should exclude any risk of pride or self-congratulation in us; his grace (gift) is acknowledged and we take no credit whatsoever for his having brought us into the Way of salvation. God's elect in Christ know that they have been brought into the Way of service, obedience and, sometimes, sacrifice. He takes us from the way of sin and death to the new Way of *life*. He calls us to *be holy* (Ephesians **1**:4–14).

As we think about God's faithful love for his faithful people and his purposes for the whole of his creation, we should be moved to echo Paul's own sense of mystery, awe and joy as expressed in Romans **11**:33 and v. 36, *Oh, the depth of the riches of the wisdom and knowledge of God! How unsearchable his judgments, and his paths beyond tracing out.......... For from him and through him and to him are all things. To him be the glory for ever! Amen.*

Further reading

[1] See Pawson, David, *Israel in the New Testament* and *Defending Christian Zionism* (Terra Nova Publications), and Jacob, Alex, *The Case for Enlargement Theology* and *Receive the Truth* (Glory to Glory Publications).

48

THE NAMES OF JESUS

Background

The Lord Jesus (*Iesous* [Greek]; *Yeshua* [Hebrew]) was given many titles, which can be seen as both affirmations of who he is and confessions of faith in him. W. Graham Scroggie, in his *Guide to the Gospels*,[1] refers to fifty-two such titles, but it is the simple name 'Jesus' by which the Lord is most often referred to in the Gospels – almost six hundred times, in fact. The name emphasises the real humanity of the Lord. Whilst to us it has become a sacred name, and many would consider it irreverent to give it to any child today (though in some Latin societies this is not an uncommon practice), in New Testament times it was one of the most common names for a boy. 'Jesus' is the name by which the Old Testament name 'Joshua' is translated. Whilst it was a common name in the first century AD, by the second century it was rapidly dying out. Among Jews it had become a hated name and among Christians it was too sacred for common use.

Ordinary though the name 'Jesus' was, it was nevertheless significant. In the ancient world a name was often seen as describing something about the person to whom it was given. It was given to our Lord by the direct instruction of God (see Matthew 1:21). Indeed, the name might have been thought somewhat irregular by people at the time as it was customary to name eldest sons after their father. We would note, in this regard, that Jesus had no biological father, so in his name may be found some clue as to his heavenly Father. The rabbis had a saying: 'Six persons received their names before they were born, namely, Isaac, our great lawgiver Moses, Solomon, Josiah, Ishmael and the Messiah.' Jewish belief was that God would directly command what the name of the Messiah must be.

In both Hebrew and Greek forms, the name Jesus has a special meaning, being in a sense, a one word summary of the work that the Lord was sent to do. In Hebrew the name 'Joshua' means, variously, 'God is my help' or 'God is rescue' or 'the help of God'. In Matthew 1:21 we read, ". . . you are to give him the name Jesus, because he will save his people from their sins." The very name Jesus, therefore, marks him out as Saviour. 'He is God's divinely appointed and divinely sent Rescuer,' writes William Barclay, 'whose function it is to deliver men from their sins. He came to rescue men from the estrangement and the alienation from God which is the consequence of their past sins, and for the future to liberate them from the bondage to sin, from the moral frustration and the continuous and inevitable defeat which are the result of sin. He came to bring friendship for fear, and victory for defeat.'[2]

To the Greek mind a connection was made between the name Jesus and the verb *iasthai*, which means to heal. The connection between the two words is only in the sound, but the Greeks made much of the idea of Jesus as the healer of the bodies and souls of men – the one who alone could bring health to the body in its physical pain and cleansing of the soul polluted by sin. It was no accident that Jesus was given his name, for it summarises the things he came to do and which *only* he could do. He came to be the divine rescuer of men from the consequences and the grip of sin.

The Son of Man

Jesus' often-used self-designation was 'Son of Man'. Used in the Gospels over 80 times, it is a reference to Daniel 7:13, *bar anash* (Aramaic, son of man; only found in this verse). Jesus applied this verse to himself in Matthew 26:64; *ben ha-adam* (Hebrew) or *uion tou anthropou* (Greek), son [of the] Man, as coming before the Ancient of Days to receive eternal dominion. *Ben enosh* (Hebrew, son of mortal man) is

used in parallel with *ben adam* (Hebrew, 'son of mankind').
See Daniel **7**:13; Psalm **144**:3; Ezekiel **2**:1; Matthew **26**:64.

The prefix 'son of' is one of four main titles of the Lord Jesus:

Son of Abraham – Matthew **1**:1; Luke **3**:34.

Son of David – Matthew **1**:1; **9**:27; **15**:22; **20**:30, 31; **21**:9, 15; **22**:42; Mark **10**:47, 48; Luke **18**:38, 39; Romans **1**:3; [and, 'I am the Root and the Offspring of David, and the bright Morning Star'; see Revelation **22**:16b].

Son of man - Matthew **8**:20; **9**:6; **10**:23; **11**:19; **12**:8, 32, 40; **13**:37, 41; **16**:27, 28; **17**:9, 12, 22; **19**:28; **20**:18, 28; **24**:27, 30, 37, 39, 44; **25**:31; **26**:2, 24, 45, 64 (see also in Mark, Luke and John); Acts **7**:56; [see also Revelation **1**:13; **14**:14, "like a son of man"].

Son of God – Matthew **4**:3, 6; **8**:29; **14**:33; **16**:16; **26**:63; **27**:40, 43, 54; Mark **1**:1; **3**:11; **15**:39; Luke **1**:35; **4**:3, 9, 41; **22**:70; John **1**:34, 49; **5**:25; **11**:27; **19**:7; **20**:31; Acts **9**:20; Romans **1**:4; 2 Corinthians **1**:19; Galatians **2**:20; Ephesians **4**:13; Hebrews **4**:14; **6**:6; **7**:3; **10**:29; 1 John **3**:8; **4**:15; **5**:1, 5, 10, 12, 13, 20; Revelation **2**:18.

Also: *Son of the Most High God* (Mark **5**:7; Luke **1**:32; **8**:28); *Son of the Blessed One* (Mark **14**:61) and *Son of Mary/ Joseph* (Mark **6**:3/John **1**:45).

Jesus has many names in Scripture, which reflect his character, nature, deity, humanity, identity, apostolic calling, mission, etc., including those listed below. [Note: Biblical references provided are intended as helpful pointers to passages for study, and there may be overlaps and multiple instances, so are neither necessarily in order nor always to complete verses, so please see the context and exact rendering in the Bible in each case; also, capitalisations may differ from those used here]:

Almighty, Author & Perfecter, Beloved, Branch, Bread of Life, Bridegroom, Bright Morning Star, Carpenter, Chosen One, Cornerstone, Counsellor, Door, Immanuel, Everlasting Father. See Hebrews **12**:2; Ephesians **1**:6 [KJV]; Isaiah **11**:1;

John **6**:35, 48; Matthew **9**:15; **25**:6; Mark **6**:3; Luke **23**:35; Isaiah **28**:16; **9**:6; John **10**:9 [KJV]; Isaiah **7**:14; Isaiah **9**:6. Also: *faithful witness, the firstborn from the dead, and the ruler of the kings of the earth* (see Revelation **1**:5); *the Amen, the faithful and true witness, the ruler of God's creation* (see Revelation **3**:14).

Firstborn, God, Head of the Church, High Priest/Apostle, Holy One, Hope, Image of God, Jesus, Judge, Lamb of God, the Lamb, Lord of lords and King of kings. See Colossians **1**:15, 18; John **1**:1; Ephesians **5**:23; Hebrews **3**:1; Mark **1**:24; 1 Timothy **1**:1; 2 Corinthians **4**:4; Matthew **1**:21; John **5**:22; **1**:29; Revelation **17**:14.

Last Adam, Light of the world, the Lion of the tribe of Judah, the Root of David, Living Water, Man of Sorrows, Master, Messenger of the Covenant, Messiah. See 1 Corinthians **15**:45; John **8**:12; Revelation **5**:5; John **4**:10; Isaiah **53**:3; Luke **8**:24; John **13**:13; Malachi **3**:1; Daniel **9**:25, 26; John **1**:41.

Mighty God, Prince of Peace, Prophet, Redeemer, Resurrection and Life, Saviour, Shepherd, Shiloh, Son of God, True Vine, The Way the Truth and the Life, Wonderful. See Isaiah **9**:6; John **6**:14; Job **19**:25; John **11**:25; Luke **2**:11; 1 Peter **2**:25; **5**:4; Genesis **49**:10; Luke **1**:35; John **15**:1; John **14**:6; Isaiah **9**:6 [KJV].

Other titles and attributes of Jesus

Scripture adds many other attributes, titles and names of the Lord Jesus, and a search for these is most rewarding as they enlighten the eyes of our heart and help us to be found in him and know him better (Ephesians **1**:18; Philippians **3**:9–10) –
The Word of God *memra* (Aramaic), *logos* (Greek), *dvar haElohim* (Hebrew); see Genesis **1**:1 (Targum Yonathan); John **1**:1, 14.
The Angel of the Lord *malach* (messenger) – see Genesis **16**:7; Exodus **3**:2; **14**:19.

The Anointed [One] *mashiach* (Hebrew, Messiah, anointed) – see Daniel **9**:25, 26 [KJV]; 1 Samuel **2**:35; Psalm **2**:2; Isaiah **61**:1; John **1**:41; **4**:25; Acts **4**:27; **10**:38.

Christ, *christos*, (Greek, anointed) is used throughout the New Testament – see Matthew **1**:1, 16; **16**:16, 20; Mark **8**:29; Luke **2**:11; **9**:20; **24**:46; John **11**:27; John **20**:31; Acts **2**:36; **3**:6, 18, 20; **4**:10; **5**:42; **9**:22; **17**:3; **18**:28 and often in Paul's letters.

Rabbi (*rav*), (Teacher, Master) – see Ecclesiastes **1**:1; Matthew **8**:19; Mark **12**:14, 19.

King (of Israel/Jews) – see Matthew **27**:42; John **1**:49; **12**:13 / Matthew **2**:2; John **19**:19.

Suffering Servant – see Psalm **22**:13–18; Isaiah **42**:1 (cf. Matthew **12**:18); Isaiah **53**:2–12; Zechariah **3**:8; Matthew **16**:21; **26**:37–38; **27**:46; **20**:18; **20**:28.

Jesus said, *"I and my Father are one"* (John **10**:30). Thus stating his identity with God's name as revealed to Moses (expressed as I AM WHO I AM or I WILL BE WHAT I WILL BE; Exodus **3**:6, 14–15, the four-letter Hebrew name YHWH), Jesus' oneness with the eternal God of Abraham, Isaac and Jacob was signified.

Jesus' "I am" statements recorded in John's Gospel are:

I AM the Bread of Life	John **6**:35, 48
I AM the [real] living Bread that came down from heaven	
	6:32, 33, 41, 51
I AM the Light of the world	**8**:12; **9**:5
I AM the Gate (Door) for the sheep	**10**:7, 9
I AM the Good shepherd	**10**:11, 14
I AM the Resurrection and the Life	**11**:25
I AM the Way, the Truth and the Life	**14**:6
I AM the True Vine	**15**:1, 5
I AM (He)	**18**:5, 6, 8
Before Abraham was born, I AM	**8**:58

Notes

Readers who want to take a fuller look at Jesus' "I am" statements free on the Glory to Glory website are directed to *The Empty Promise of Godism* Chapter 9 and Appendix 2 – both downloadable as PDF files.

[1] W. Graham Scroggie DD, *A Guide To The Gospels* (Pickering & Inglis Ltd, 1948) p. 519.
[2] William Barclay, *Jesus As They Saw Him* (SCM Press Ltd, 1962) p. 12.

49

THE SUFFERING CHURCH

Background

The people of God are familiar with persecution. The entire Holy Bible is a testament not only to God's goodness, justice and mercy, but also to the devil's opposition to God, which manifests itself in opposition to God's people in particular, and to all humankind in general. Right back in the earliest parts of the Bible we see persecution of the righteous by the unrighteous. 'Righteousness' is a word that the world does not like. 'Righteousness' seen from a human perspective is living as God intended. It always involves faith as we can never achieve righteousness by our own efforts. Righteousness comes from faith in Jesus Christ, crucified and risen. Righteousness is in contrast to (and in opposition to) evil. Evil will not countenance righteousness but opposes it.

We focus in this Study on suffering in the context of persecution. Jesus said, *Blessed are you when people insult you, persecute you and falsely say all kinds of evil against you because of me. Rejoice and be glad, because great is your reward in heaven, for in the same way they persecuted the prophets who were before you* (Matthew **5**:11–12).

The Old Testament

The earliest persecution that we encounter in the Bible was of Abel by his brother Cain, in Genesis chapter 4. Abel's sacrifice was acceptable to God, whilst Cain's sacrifice was not. So Cain was greatly jealous of Abel and murdered him – persecution to the point of death. (See Matthew **23**:35; 1 John **3**:12–13.)

The persecution of Lot and his two visitors is not typical of the persecution found in the Bible. Persecution is normally experienced over long periods of time. The persecution of Lot and his visitors was over a short period and yet it reminds us of what often happens in this world when whole communities gather, mob-handed, to persecute the righteous (Genesis **19**:1– 9). The fact that Lot is called a 'foreigner' suggests that hostility to him may have predated the incident recorded in Genesis **19**.

The persecution of the Hebrews recorded in the book of Exodus was first and foremost because they were God's chosen people. It seems that Satan was seeking to prevent the people of God from reaching their promised land. The attempts to oppress them (Exodus **5**:1–21) were ultimately aimed at destroying them, which became the candid objective of Pharaoh's pursuit of them with an army (Exodus **14**:5–9). Whilst the incessant troubles recorded in the book of Judges, and Samuel, and Kings, might be considered by some as the ebb and flow of nations and tribes in conflict, the constant attack of Israel by its neighbours and those who lived among them also seems to have a deeper spiritual context. We are shown, especially in Isaiah, that some of Israel's troubles stemmed from faithlessness and disobedience. It is clear, however, that some of the faithful (like the prophet Isaiah) suffered in this world for being true to God and speaking his word boldly. The letter to the Hebrews lists some of the faithful witnesses who had suffered in the past.

The New Testament

It is in the New Testament that the reality of persecution of the disciples of Jesus – and in that we mean the true church (see Study 26) – becomes much clearer.

In John **15**:18–21, Jesus said, *If the world hates you, keep in mind that it hated me first. If you belonged to the world, it would love you as its own. As it is, you do not belong to the world, but I have chosen you out of the world. That is why the world hates you. Remember the words I spoke to you: 'No* *servant is greater than his master.' If they persecuted me, they will persecute you also. If they obeyed my teaching, they will obey yours also. They will treat you this way because of my name ....'* And then in John **16**:1–2, *All this I have told you so that you will not go astray. They will put you out of the synagogue; in fact, a time is coming when anyone who kills you will think he is offering a service to God.* In saying that, Jesus was addressing the persecution that would afflict the immediate disciples and the early church. But he was also addressing all those who follow him. What was true for the disciples then is true for us today, but not always in such extremes.

Our Lord Jesus repeatedly warned of persecution for those who follow him, even within households – that brother would betray brother and children would betray parents. Jesus pointed out that even the Son of Man had nowhere to lay his head (Matthew **8**:20) so his followers should not expect an easy ride. Jesus told us not to be afraid when arraigned before the courts – the Holy Spirit will give us the words we need to say in our defence, and just as pertinently, we might add, in Jesus' defence as well. Luke records Jesus as saying, *...they will lay hands on you and persecute you. They will deliver you to synagogues and prisons, and you will be brought before kings and governors, and all on account of my name. This will result in your being witnesses to them. But make up your mind not to worry beforehand how you will defend yourselves. For I will give you words and wisdom that none of your adversaries will be able to resist or contradict* (Luke **21**:12–15). In Matthew chapter 10 Jesus also warns of persecutions to come (Matthew **10**:21–39).

The Lord himself is the ultimate realist. He knew what his own death would be. He made it very clear that to follow him is no picnic – it never has been and never will be easy. On account of Jesus, strife will emerge within societies, within friendships, and even within families. So, Jesus' call to discipleship includes frank warnings of danger, and of reviling, slander, accusation, floggings, arraignment before courts, hatred and death. There is a high cost to following

Jesus. The Lord himself would be judicially murdered on false accusations of subversion, of forbidding the payment of taxes and of claiming to be king. Each accusation was a lie, but this did not protect him.

In the book of Acts we encounter the first persecutions against the fledgling church. But – and we need always to keep this very much in mind – God is in control. The early church was scattered by persecution, and the gospel message – of a righteous God of grace whose Son Jesus died and rose again that we might live – spread ever further. The whole epistle of 1 Peter is about preparing for suffering by way of persecution. (See 1 Peter **4**:12–19.)

Jesus spoke clearly of the cost that would be incurred by becoming one of his disciples, and around the world today the body of Christ is experiencing great persecution. God commands us to remember them and pray for them as if we were suffering right beside them – see, e.g., Hebrews **13**:3.

God will preserve for himself a church and a holy nation in spite of persecution suffered by his children. And those martyred men, women and children – martyred as they have been down through history – will have a special place in the kingdom of heaven. Where do we find the end of this story? As we might expect, it is at the end of the Bible. We pick up the story in Revelation chapter **6**, where the apostle John recounts his vision of heaven's seals being opened. When the fifth seal is opened, John saw, ...*the souls of those who had been slain because of the word of God and the testimony they had maintained.* They ask God openly how long it will be before their blood is avenged. They are told to wait a little longer, until the last of the martyrs are gathered to heaven. Then, in chapter **7** we see the glorious climax. One of the elders said, *These are they who have come out of the great tribulation; they have washed their robes and made them white in the blood of the Lamb. Therefore, they are before the throne of God and serve him day and night in his temple; and he who sits on the throne will spread his tent over them. Never again will they hunger; never again will they thirst. The sun will not beat upon them, nor any* *scorching heat. For the Lamb at the centre of the throne will be their shepherd; he will lead them to springs of living water. And God will wipe away every tear from their eyes.* (See Revelation **7**:13ff.)

Finally, in Revelation chapter **19**, John recounts: *Then I heard what sounded like a great multitude, like the roar of rushing waters and like loud peals of thunder, shouting: "Hallelujah! For our Lord God Almighty reigns. Let us rejoice and be glad and give him the glory! For the wedding of the Lamb has come, and his bride has made herself ready. Fine linen, bright and clean, was given her to wear." (Fine linen stands for the righteous acts of the saints.) Then the angel said to me, "Write: 'Blessed are those who are invited to the wedding supper of the Lamb!'" And he added, "These are the true words of God"* (Revelation **19**:6–9).

Summary

Although persecution of Christians is inevitable, it is also a means of blessing for those who suffer it. The persecution of Jesus' disciples is linked in the Gospels with the labour pains of the age to come (Matthew **24**:4–12). Those who are persecuted for the sake of righteousness are promised the kingdom of heaven (Matthew **5**:10). Paul affirms that those who suffer with Messiah Jesus will also be glorified with him (Romans **8**:17).

These blessings are not only for the future: suffering produces perseverance, character and hope in this life, so that believers can even rejoice in it (Romans **5**:3–4; James **1**:2–3). These blessings may pass from those who are persecuted to their brothers and sisters in Christ: it enables Christians to comfort other believers with the comfort they have received from God (2 Corinthians **1**:3–7). Paul's afflictions are presented as his sharing in Christ's sufferings for the sake of the church (Colossians **1**:24). And he also bears witness to his endurance of persecution for the sake of Messiah (2 Corinthians **4**:8–12; **6**:4–10; **11**:23–25), a response required elsewhere from all God's people (Revelation **13**:10).

Jesus' disciples are not left alone to face their enemies. Jesus himself will provide them with the words and wisdom to defend themselves (Luke **21**:12–15). No one can snatch them out of his, or the Father's hand (John **10**:28–29) – provided they stand firm to the end, they will be saved (Matthew **24**:13).

50

EVIDENCE THAT JESUS IS ALIVE TODAY

Background

The Christian faith is unlike all other faiths. This is evident, for example, in the unique way that Christian believers can know assurance of forgiveness of sins (see Unit 9), and can know personally the reality of *abiding in Christ*, having life in him. In this closing Study we stress the uniqueness of our faith, and the universality of its claims. These arise from the living person of Jesus Christ (*Yeshua* the Messiah), whose life, claims, teaching and actions (as well as the apostolic witness to him) have eternal significance because he is alive now – not a dead teacher, but actually reigning in glory, true God and true Man, the second person of the Holy Trinity.

If Jesus Christ had not been raised from the dead (leaving behind an empty tomb, as he did) there would be no Christianity today, and none of the benefits of his life, miracles, suffering and death would be available to anyone now.

We have touched briefly on this theme elsewhere in these Studies, especially in Unit 14 (Death – Physical). But it is essential for our own witness that we have a clear grasp of the evidence which we can present confidently to others.

We will never 'argue' anyone into becoming a believer, but it is our duty and privilege to declare and to witness to certain facts. From the outset, our faith has been *historical*, meaning followers of 'the Way' have known that certain things have *really happened in certain times and places*, which are attested by those who were physically there and observed what occurred. So there are essential historical claims that we can make with confidence, and they are an important part of our presentation of the good news. These facts were recorded (orally and in writing) and could have been disproved if they had been untrue. It is scarcely credible that anyone would have been willing to have been tortured and risk being judicially murdered for a tissue of lies and fabrication of their own devising! Yet in effect this is what those who deny the reality of the resurrection ask people to believe. The futility of a belief system which denies the resurrection of Jesus from the dead is made clear in 1 Corinthians **15**:19.

The Old Testament

It would be surprising if the OT did not prepare the people of God for the most momentous event in history.

Old Testament saints anticipated a resurrection of their bodies. See Job **19**:26–27; Psalm **49**:15; **71**:20; see also John **11**:24. It is interesting that Matthew **27**:51 records that at the death of Jesus many holy people who had died were raised to life.

The resurrection of the Messiah was prophesied in Psalm **16**:8–11 (see Acts **2**:25–31). In Psalm **22** (from the opening of which our Lord quoted on the cross) we can see the victory and dominion of the Messiah. See also Isaiah chapter **53**, Acts **17**:2–3; **26**:22–23. Nevertheless, John **20**:9 records that even at the time of discovering the empty tomb there were disciples who did not yet understand from Scripture (the Old Testament) that Jesus had to rise from the dead.

The New Testament

The centrality and the absolutely vital character of the historical claim that Jesus rose from the dead is clearly asserted by the apostle Paul in 1 Corinthians **15**. The whole chapter should be read. The saving death, burial and resurrection are all linked in the opening verses. (1– 5). Then begins a record of many eyewitnesses: Cephas (Peter) and the twelve (v. 5); then 'over five hundred brothers at one time'. Importantly, from the point of view of contemporary historical verification, it is stated that the 'majority' of those people who had seen Jesus after his death were still alive (v. 6). Then James and other apostles are cited as witnesses (v. 7), followed by Paul himself. That is an extremely impressive assembly of witnesses who were perfectly able to testify to the personal experience of seeing Jesus alive after his death and burial. Any sceptic could have asked them exactly what they saw and, again we note that witnessing to what they had seen was an extremely risky business. Why would they have taken such a risk if they were lying?

In the Gospels and Acts we have a wealth of further eyewitness evidence.

Matthew **28**:1–20; Mark **16**:9–20 (even if an addition to Mark, this is still inspired Holy Scripture); Luke **24**:1–53; John **20**:1– **21**:25.

Acts **1**:1-9 records conversation between the risen Lord and disciples prior to the Ascension and Pentecost. In the course of that conversation, the disciples show by their questioning that they have a clear hope and expectation of Jesus' return to rule Israel (see v. 6). Jesus does not rebuke them or deny that their hope is valid. He explains to them that the Father knows. This, like all the other passages cited, has a very clear 'ring of truth', in that this is precisely the kind of concern which expectant Jews, the Lord's disciples, would have had.

The restoration of Peter, following his denial of Christ, is so characteristic of the same Lord Jesus to whom the Gospels testify concerning the *whole* of Jesus' earthly ministry: the compassion, the opportunity given for repentance, and the re-commissioning of Peter.

The appearance of Jesus to the women, again, is so clearly the Lord himself. He asked Mary, one of the many witnesses, not to cling to him (John **20**:17). How consistent and understandable that was, in the light of the Ascension which was to follow. She and the other believers would be able to know the Spirit's presence and power soon after that.

Again and again, the 'ring of truth' is there in every encounter between the risen Lord Jesus and the people who saw him in his risen body. All of this is historical fact based on contemporaneous eyewitness accounts by many people – of both sexes and from many walks of life.

Personal testimony evidence in every age, including the present day

There are countless published testimonies by people today and in the past who have recorded personal encounters with Jesus Christ – often through experiences of changed lives, answered prayer, extraordinary 'co-incidences', signs and miracles. Some have visions and dreams. Some people may hear an audible or an inner 'voice'. Some of these kinds of encounter may require confirmation before action is based on them, but *every* true Christian has encountered the same Lord Jesus who died and is now alive, for we live in him and he dwells in his people.

Conclusion

In closing, we note that the significance of the resurrection extends far beyond the matter of proof that there is life after death. Here are just a few key things which flow from the well-attested resurrection of Jesus Christ from the dead, all of which are of great significance to every believer:

(1) In raising Jesus from the dead, God the Father vindicated him. (See Hebrews **10**:12.) The verdicts of the Jewish and Roman courts have been overturned by God. Jesus was not blaspheming when he claimed to be divine, he was telling the truth. He was not committing treason in the matter of kingship. He really *is* the King of kings.

(2) In the resurrection of Jesus, the new creation has begun and believers are part of God's new creation. (See 2 Corinthians **5**:17.)

(3) Everything Jesus ever said and did was true and remains true. He is the way, the truth and the life (see John **14**:6). All that he foretold will really happen. He will return to judge the living and the dead (see John **5**:22).

(4) His sacrifice for our sins has been accepted, so we can be forgiven on the basis of faith in him. (See again Hebrews **10**:12–39.)

THE WORD OF THE LORD IS LIKE . . .

In these passages we learn something of the meanings and rich significance of the expression 'word of God'

The Bible is like a double-edged sword
Hebrews **4**:12 – For the word of God is living and active. Sharper than any double-edged sword, it penetrates even to dividing soul and spirit, joints and marrow; it judges the thoughts and attitudes of the heart.

Like fire and a hammer
Jeremiah **23**:29 – "Is not my word like fire," declares the LORD, "and **like a hammer** that breaks a rock in pieces?"

Like a lamp and a light
Psalm **119**:105 – Your word is a lamp to my feet, and a light for my path.

Like food
Matthew **4**:4 – "Man does not live on bread alone, but on every word that comes from the mouth of God."

1 Peter **1**:25–**2**:2 "But the word of the Lord stands forever." And this is the word that was preached to you. Therefore, rid yourselves of all malice and all deceit, hypocrisy, envy, and slander of every kind. Like newborn babies, crave pure spiritual milk, so that by it you may grow up in your salvation."

Like seed which is sown
Mark **4**:20 – "Others, like seed sown on good soil, hear the word, accept it, and produce a crop—some thirty, some sixty, some a hundred times what was sown."

Is instrumental in new birth
1 Peter **1**:23 – For you have been born again, not of perishable seed, but of imperishable, through the living and enduring word of God.

Like a mirror
James **1**:22–25 – Do not merely listen to the word, and so deceive yourselves. Do what it says. Anyone who listens to the word but does not do what it says is like a man who looks at his face in a mirror and, after looking at himself, goes away and immediately forgets what he looks like. But the man who looks intently into the perfect law that gives freedom, and continues to do this, not forgetting what he has heard, but doing it — he will be blessed in what he does.

---

www.glorytoglory.co.uk